At the Foot of the Mountain

At the Foot of the Mountain

Two Views on Torah and the Spirit

JOSHUA M. LESSARD
JENNIFER M. ROSNER

Foreword by David Rudolph

RESOURCE *Publications* • Eugene, Oregon

AT THE FOOT OF THE MOUNTAIN
Two Views on Torah and the Spirit

Copyright © 2021 Joshua M. Lessard and Jennifer M. Rosner. All rights reserved. Except for brief quotations in critical publications or reviews, no part of this book may be reproduced in any manner without prior written permission from the publisher. Write: Permissions, Wipf and Stock Publishers, 199 W. 8th Ave., Suite 3, Eugene, OR 97401.

Resource Publications
An Imprint of Wipf and Stock Publishers
199 W. 8th Ave., Suite 3
Eugene, OR 97401

www.wipfandstock.com

PAPERBACK ISBN: 978-1-6667-0063-3
HARDCOVER ISBN: 978-1-6667-0064-0
EBOOK ISBN: 978-1-6667-0065-7

06/03/21

CONTENTS

Foreword by David Rudolph	vii
Introduction	1
October 17, 2018	5
October 24, 2018	10
October 29, 2018	13
November 4, 2018	20
November 11, 2018	25
November 19, 2018	32
November 23, 2018	36
November 28, 2018	44
December 3, 2018	47
January 6, 2018	53
January 8, 2019	58
January 14, 2019	65
January 24, 2019	71
April 30, 2019	81
May 8, 2019	87
May 20, 2019	94
Concluding Reflections	99
Addendum: Two Views on Torah in Matthew 5:17–20	112
Bibliography	119

FOREWORD

There is a Jewish proverb that sometimes comes to mind when I think of the Messianic Jewish community—*Hasavlanut—machatzeet hayedee'a* ("Patience is already halfway to knowledge"). The modern Messianic movement has come a long way over the past 250 years,[1] and yet there are a number of foundational areas related to the spirituality and identity of the movement that we are still trying to get a handle on. One of these areas is the focus of this book—the relationship between the Spirit and Torah in Messianic Judaism. In order to fully appreciate the conversation around this topic in the chapters ahead, it is important to understand some of the historical and ecclesial background leading up to it.

The twenty-first century Messianic Jewish community has its origins in first, an outpouring of the Spirit on the Jewish people in the 1960s and 1970s that led to the emergence of over 500 Messianic synagogues in a fifty-year period, and second, a Jewish renewal movement within the church that since the mid-eighteenth century has advocated for the importance of Messianic Jews and their children retaining their Torah-defined Jewish identity on the basis of covenant and calling. This is all to say that the Spirit and Torah are central to the Messianic Jewish movement's past, present and—I would suggest—future.

The three largest Messianic Jewish organizations in the world that represent Messianic Jews and Messianic synagogues reflect this focus on the Spirit and Torah to varying degrees. The Messianic Jewish Alliance of America (MJAA) and its congregational counterpart—the International Alliance of Messianic Congregations and Synagogues (IAMCS)—give voice to the principal role of the Spirit in Messianic Judaism and see Spirit-initiated revival as critical to

---

1. See Rudolph, "Messianic Judaism," 21–36.

the Messianic movement fulfilling its *raison d'être*. The Spirit, they contend, points Jews back to a walk with God primarily guided by his Word rather than tradition:

> The modern messianic Jewish movement is a move of God's Spirit, which is restoring Israel to a faith that is based in the Bible, not in the sayings of the Rabbis. The prophetic, end-time salvation of Israel is unfolding, and it is a blessing for the whole world. The vision of the IAMCS is to see the outpouring of God's Spirit upon the Jewish people.[2]

Here we are reminded that Messianic Judaism is inherently a Messiah-centered, Bible-based, Spirit-empowered expression of Judaism and that the Messianic movement defines itself to some extent in contradistinction to traditional Judaism. Along these lines, the IAMCS calls into question "the essential premise of rabbinic authority."[3] In their publication *The Non-Torah: Exposing the Mythology of Divine Oral Torah*, the IAMCS describes the traditional Jewish narrative of an oral Torah given on Mount Sinai and later rabbis appointed by God to be its authoritative interpreters as "the foundation stone upon which the house of Rabbinic Judaism is built."[4] While honoring the wisdom of the sages, and the value of traditional Jewish customs,[5] the MJAA/IAMCS views the rabbinic construction and implementation of a divinely sanctioned oral Torah to be something that makes Rabbinic Judaism fundamentally off-course and inconsistent with Messianic Judaism:

---

2. International Alliance of Messianic Congregations and Synagogues (IAMCS), *The Non-Torah,* back cover. The first line of the IAMCS's "Our Vision" statement declares, "The spiritual vision of the IAMCS is to see the outpouring of G-d's Spirit upon our Jewish people through Messianic congregations."

3. IAMCS, *The Non-Torah*, 34, 37.

4. IAMCS, *The Non-Torah*, 129.

5. "Tradition, culture and religious law made by the rabbis was indeed transmitted generationally. Some of it is good, some not so good. Some of it is outright bad. In any case, it isn't God's word. Accordingly, while Rabbinic tradition is embraced by Messianic Jews, it is with the understanding that tradition is part of the fabric of our lives. But it is not Torah" (IAMCS, *The Non-Torah*, 36; see also 34–35, 37, 128, 156–57).

Foreword

> There is no way to harmonize oral Torah theology with faith in Yeshua . . . The Rabbis have maintained the posture of rejecting Yeshua for nearly two millennia, and all the while maintaining that the oral Torah gives them the authority to say so on behalf of all Israel . . . After all, if God gave Moses the future halakha at Sinai, surely God also gave Moses the ruling of the Sanhedrin which rejected Yeshua, along with all future halakha that has maintained that future rejection for the last two millennia . . . Every Jew who accepts Yeshua as Messiah inevitably hears "but the Rabbis say Yeshua can't be the Messiah!" Indeed, the Rabbis say Yeshua is not the Messiah. But the Scriptures declare the truth that He is Messiah. The Rabbis say they are the ones who have authority to say who is the Messiah . . . If Yeshua is Messiah then it's game over for orthodox Rabbinic Judaism. Because if He is Messiah, then the whole halakhic ship is sunk. Halakha would become at best advisory, but clearly not a revelation from God to Moses.[6]

For the IAMCS, Rabbinic Judaism not only lacks the authority it claims to make *halakha* (Jewish law) and calls Jewish people to reject Israel's own Messiah but it also misses the mark in elevating *halakha* to a place where rabbinic decisions are at times viewed as God's Word.[7] When this imbalance is brought into the Messianic community, the IAMCS has observed that it tends to result in bad fruit:

> Since the late 1960's and 1970's, there have been those who have tried to interject orthodox rabbinic Judaism into the context of the Messianic Jewish revival. It has been well-established over the last forty to fifty years that any of these kinds of efforts which make "Torah" the issue, never seem to lead anywhere good. Oftentimes, they give rise to controversies, factionalism, and division.[8]

As an example of *halakha* raised to the level of God's Word, consider the custom of lighting *Chanukah* candles. During this eight-day

---

6. IAMCS, *The Non-Torah*, 131–32, 135.
7. IAMCS, *The Non-Torah*, 21–23, 34.
8. IAMCS, *The Non-Torah*, 144.

holiday, our family uses a traditional *siddur* and recites blessings before kindling the *Chanukkiyah*. The traditional opening blessing is:

> Blessed are You, *Hashem* our God, King of the universe, Who has sanctified us with His commandments, and commanded us to kindle the *Chanukah* light.

But did God really *command* us to light the *Chanukah* lights? Meir Zlotowitz, an Orthodox Jewish rabbi and founder of ArtScroll Publications, addresses this question directly:

> *And commanded us to kindle the Chanukah light.* This is the text of this blessing as recorded in the Talmud (*Shabbos* 23a). The Talmud proceeds to record the obvious question: "Where did He command us?" That is, since the kindling of the Chanukah light is of post-Biblical origin and ordained by the Sages of the pre-Mishnaic period, how can we imply that God *Himself* commanded us to kindle these lights, as if it were ordained by the Torah? The Talmud explains that the Torah commands us to follow the ordinances of the recognized Torah leaders—*you shall not turn aside from the sentence which they shall show you* [*Deut.* 17:11]. Accordingly, a Rabbinic observance—such as the requirement to kindle lights on Chanukah—has Biblical sanction, and the term *v'tzivanu, and he has commanded us,* is quite appropriate.[9]

The implication of Rabbi Zlotowitz's (and the Talmud's) explanation is that in order to recite the first *Chanukah* blessing with *kavana* (that is, intention or direction of the heart) one has to acknowledge the authority of the rabbis to add to God's commandments, i.e., to place *halakha* on the level of God's Word. Personally, I find this highly problematic,[10] which is why our family respectfully modifies the blessing and says:

---

9. Zlotowitz, *Chanukah*, 124.

10. "[T]he decision-making authority of the judges described in Deut 17:8–13 is to take the law of God and apply it to matters of controversy. The verse emphasizes the importance of respecting the decisions that they make. That is not to say that the word of these *shoftim* or judges is equivalent to the Word of God. The fact that Deut 17:11 says: '*You are to act according to the instruction they teach you and the judgment they tell you—you must not turn*

Foreword

> Blessed are You, *Hashem* our God, King of the universe, Who has sanctified us with His commandments, *and put it in our hearts [va'asher natan b'libenu] to kindle the Chanukah light.*[11]

These words I can say sincerely because my wife, Harumi, and I sense a leading of God's Spirit to kindle the *Chanukah* light in our home. It is not a matter of Torah but *Ruach HaKodesh* (the Holy Spirit). My point in sharing our family tradition, and the reason behind it, is to underscore that the IAMCS makes a reasonable point when it raises concerns about the level of authority that Rabbinic Judaism attributes to *halakha* and how this can be squared with the Messianic Jewish view that rabbis can interpret God's commandments but not create them (Deut 4:2; 12:32).

The third largest umbrella organization in the Messianic movement is the Union of Messianic Jewish Congregations (UMJC). In contrast to the MJAA/IAMCS, the Union, while agreeing with the Alliance that the oral Torah was not given on Mount Sinai, gives more weight to the importance of Torah and Jewish tradition in Messianic Judaism. This is reflected in the organization's governing documents. For example, in the UMJC's "Our Values" statement, the first core value listed is "Unity in Diversity." In this context, the "ongoing significance of the Torah for Jewish life" is emphasized:

> The UMJC represents diverse congregations united in our commitment to the authority of Scripture as the Word of God, the ongoing significance of the Torah for Jewish life, and the centrality of Yeshua as Lord and

---

aside from it,' is meant in the context that the judges are applying the written law to everyday life. It does not mean that there is an oral Torah that they have as well, involving many laws given by God which are not recorded in what Moses wrote down in the Torah. Furthermore, it does not mean that whatever they say, whether written here in the Torah or not, is to be considered the Word of God" (IAMCS, *The Non-Torah*, 116–17).

11. This substitution draws on the language of Exod 35:34 and Ezra 7:27. For the Shabbat blessing, we retain *v'tzivanu* and replace *l'hadlik ner shel Shabbat* (to kindle the Sabbath light) with *lishmor v'lizkor et-yom haShabbat* (to keep and remember the day of Shabbat), drawing on the language of God's commandment in Exod 20:6 and Deut 5:12 as reflected in *Lecha Dodi*.

Messiah. Deference and respect are key elements in our fellowship.[12]

Notably, the Spirit is *not* mentioned in any of the five values. Similarly, Torah and tradition are highlighted in the UMJC's "Defining Messianic Judaism: Basic Statement" but there is no explicit mention of the Spirit:

> Messianic Judaism is a movement of Jewish congregations and groups committed to Yeshua the Messiah that embrace the covenantal responsibility of Jewish life and identity rooted in Torah, expressed in tradition, and renewed and applied in the context of the New Covenant.[13]

While "in the context of the New Covenant" likely suggests an important role of the Spirit, this is not explained anywhere, even in the "Defining Messianic Judaism: Expanded Statement" which explicitly reiterates the importance of Torah and tradition:

> In the Messianic Jewish way of life, we seek to fulfill Israel's covenantal responsibility embodied in the Torah within a New Covenant context. Messianic Jewish halakhah is rooted in Scripture (Tanakh and the New Covenant writings), which is of unique sanctity and authority. It also draws upon Jewish tradition, especially those practices and concepts that have won near-universal acceptance by devout Jews through the centuries. Furthermore, as is common within Judaism, Messianic Judaism recognizes that halakhah is and must be dynamic, involving the application of the Torah to a wide variety of changing situations and circumstances. Messianic Judaism embraces the fullness of New Covenant realities available through Yeshua, and seeks to express them in forms drawn from Jewish experience and accessible to Jewish people.[14]

In the UMJC "Statement of Faith," Torah is mentioned 6 times (with a paragraph focusing on Torah under the category "Messianic

---

12. UMJC, "Values."
13. UMJC, "Defining."
14. UMJC, "Defining."

Jewish Life"),[15] the Spirit 3 times, and tradition 2 times.[16] By contrast, the MJAA "Statement of Faith" mentions the Spirit 12 times (with two paragraphs focusing on the Spirit under the category "God the Holy Spirit [*Ruach HaKodesh*]"). In the MJAA statement, there is no explicit mention of the Torah or tradition.[17]

UMJC leaders have written extensively on the topic of Torah and tradition while leaving a gap when it comes to guidance on the role of the Spirit in Messianic Jewish life:

Torah & Messianic Judaism

- Michael Rudolph with Daniel C. Juster, *The Law of Messiah: Torah from a New Covenant Perspective*. 2 vols. Montgomery Village: Tikkun International, 2019.

- Mark S. Kinzer, "The Helsinki Consultation on Jewish Continuity in the Body of Messiah: Introduction to the Berlin Statement on the Torah." *Kesher: A Journal of Messianic Judaism* 27 (2013): 83–87.

- Mark S. Kinzer, "The Torah and Jews in the Christian Church: Covenantal Calling and Pragmatic Practice." Helsinki Consultation on Jewish Continuity in the Body of Messiah, Berlin, June 29–July 3, 2012.

- Stuart Dauermann, "Jewish Believers in Yeshua and Halachic Torah Observance: Whether, What, and How?" Pages 187–204 in *Chosen to Follow: Jewish Believers through History and Today*. Edited by Knut H. Hoyland and Jakob W. Nielsen.

---

15. "The Torah is God's gift to Israel. It serves as the constitution of the Jewish people and thus also of the Messianic Jewish community, which comprises Israel's eschatological firstfruits [sic]. The Torah does not have the same role for Messianic communities from the nations, though it does provide spiritual nourishment as a witness to the Messiah. The Torah also provides universal norms of behavior and practical life teaching for all. The Torah is to be applied anew in every generation, and in this age as is fitting to the New Covenant order (Matt 5:17–20; 2 Tim 3:16–17; 1 Cor 7:17–20)" (UMJC, "Statement").

16. See UMJC, "Statement."

17. See MJAA, "Statement."

Jerusalem: Caspari Center for Biblical and Jewish Studies, 2012.

- David J. Rudolph, "Paul's 'Rule in All the Churches' (1 Cor 7:17–24) and Torah-Defined Ecclesiological Variegation." *Studies in Christian-Jewish Relations* 5:1 (2010): 1–24.

- Barney Kasdan, *God's Appointed Times: A Practical Guide for Understanding and Celebrating the Biblical Holidays*. Clarksville: Lederer, 2007.

- Russell Resnik, *Creation to Completion: A Guide to Life's Journey from the Five Books of Moses*. Clarksville: Lederer, 2006.

- *First Steps in Messianic Jewish Ethics: Defining Our Involvement with One Another and the World About Us*. Hashivenu Forum, 2013.

- Mark S. Kinzer, "Scripture and Tradition." Pages 29–37 in *Voices of Messianic Judaism: Confronting Critical Issues Facing a Maturing Movement*. Edited by Dan Cohn-Sherbok. Baltimore: Lederer, 2001.

- Russell Resnik, "Halakhic Responsibility." Pages 39–46 in *Voices of Messianic Judaism: Confronting Critical Issues Facing a Maturing Movement*. Edited by Dan Cohn-Sherbok. Baltimore: Lederer, 2001.

- David Friedman, *They Loved the Torah: What Yeshua's First Followers Really Thought about the Law*. Clarksville: Lederer, 2001.

- Russell Resnik, *Gateways to Torah: Joining the Ancient Conversation on the Weekly Portion*. Baltimore: Lederer, 2000.

- Barney Kasdan, *God's Appointed Customs: A Messianic Jewish Guide to the Biblical Lifecycle and Lifestyle*. Clarksville: Lederer, 1996.

- Daniel C. Juster, "Messianic Judaism and the Torah." Pages 113–121 in *Jewish Identity and Faith in Jesus*. Edited by Kai Kjaer-Hansen. Jerusalem: Caspari Center for Biblical and Jewish Studies, 1996.

FOREWORD

Tradition & Messianic Judaism

- *Siddur Kehillat Zera Avraham: Morning Service for Shabbat, Festival Amidah, Hallel.* Ann Arbor: Congregation Zera Avraham, 2020.
- *Siddur Kehillat Zera Avraham: Erev Shabbat, Zichron Mashiach, Havdalah.* Ann Arbor: Congregation Zera Avraham, 2020.
- *Machzor Kehillat Zera Avraham: Rosh Hashanah.* Ann Arbor: Congregation Zera Avraham, 2020.
- *Machzor Kehillat Zera Avraham: Yom Kippur.* Ann Arbor: Congregation Zera Avraham, 2020.
- *Siddur Kehillat Zera Avraham: Evening Service for Tisha B'Av.* Ann Arbor: Congregation Zera Avraham, 2020.
- Daniel C. Juster, *New Covenant Siddur: A Yeshua-Centered Messianic Jewish Worship Book.* Frederick: Tikkun America, 2019.
- Kirk Gliebe, ed., *A Messianic Jewish Siddur for Shabbat and Festivals.* Translated by Barry A. Budoff. Skokie: Devar Emet Messianic Publications, 2017.
- Messianic Jewish Rabbinical Council, "Standards of Observance." MJRC, 2014.
- Carl Kinbar, "Messianic Jews and Jewish Tradition." Pages 72–81 in *Introduction to Messianic Judaism: Its Ecclesial Context and Biblical Foundations.* Edited by David Rudolph and Joel Willitts. Grand Rapids: Zondervan, 2013.
- Seth N. Klayman, "Reflections of the Role of Torah and Jewish Tradition at Congregation Sha'arei Shalom." Pages 65–84 in *The Borough Park Papers: Symposium III: How Jewish Should the Messianic Jewish Community Be? October 22–24, 2012.* Clarksville: Messianic Jewish Publishers, 2013.
- Joshua Brumbach, "Helpful Points to Consider: The Role of Torah and Jewish Tradition in the Messianic Jewish Community." Pages 51–64 in *The Borough Park Papers: Symposium III: How*

Jewish Should the Messianic Jewish Community Be? October 22–24, 2012. Clarksville: Messianic Jewish Publishers, 2013.

- Daniel C. Juster, "Extra-Biblical Practices" and "Dangers to be Faced." Pages 287–302, 313–17 in *Jewish Roots: Understanding Your Jewish Faith*. Revised Edition. Shippensburg: Destiny Image, 2013.

- Mark S. Kinzer, "Messianic Judaism and Jewish Tradition in the Twenty-First Century: A Biblical Defense of Oral Torah." Pages 29–61 in Mark S. Kinzer, *Israel's Messiah and the People of God: A Vision for Messianic Jewish Covenantal Identity*. Edited by Jennifer M. Rosner. Eugene: Cascade, 2011.

- Carl Kinbar, "Israel, Torah, and the Knowledge of God: Engaging the Jewish Conversation." *Kesher: A Journal of Messianic Judaism* 24 (2010): 1–28.

- Mark S. Kinzer, "Jewish Tradition and the Christological Test" and "Jewish Tradition and the Biblical Test." Pages 213–62 in *Postmissionary Messianic Judaism: Redefining Christian Engagement with the Jewish People*. Grand Rapids: Brazos, 2005.

- Michael H. Schiffman, "Messianic Judaism and Jewish Tradition in the 21st Century: A Historical Perspective on 'Oral Torah.'" Hashivenu Forum, 2003.

- Daniel C. Juster, "The Value of Tradition." Hashivenu Forum, 2003.

- John Fischer, "The Place of Rabbinic Tradition in a Messianic Jewish Lifestyle." Pages 145–70 in *The Enduring Paradox: Exploratory Essays in Messianic Judaism*. Clarksville: Messianic Jewish Publishers, 2000.

- Kay Silberling, Paal Saal, Elazar Brandt, and David J. Rudolph. "Forum: Oral Tradition and New Covenant Scripture." *Kesher: A Journal of Messianic Judaism* 8 (1999): 39–59.

- Stuart Dauermann, "Transmitting Tradition: The Biblical and Jewish Mandate." *Kesher: A Journal of Messianic Judaism* 1 (1994): 155–79.

Foreword

- John Fischer, *Messianic Services for the Festivals & Holy Days*. Palm Harbor: Menorah Ministries, 1992.
- John Fischer and David Bronstein, *Siddur for Messianic Jews*. Palm Harbor: Menorah Ministries, 1988.

The Spirit & Messianic Judaism

- Michael Rudolph, "Welcoming the Ruach HaKodesh in Jewish Space." Pages 211–15 in *Collected Sermons and Writings: On Subjects Useful for Bible Studies and Practical Godly Living*. Vol. 1. Frederick: Tikkun America, 2020.
- Michael Rudolph, "Liturgy, Holy Spirit, and Time." Pages 452–53 in *Collected Sermons and Writings I*.
- David Tokajer, *Spirit + Truth: Rediscovering the Holy Spirit from Creation through Today*. Daphne: David Tokajer, 2019.
- Carl Kinbar, "For the Common Good." Pages 19–37 in *Gifts of the Spirit: Complete Conference Lectures*. Marshfield: FFOZ, 2013.
- Daniel C. Juster, "The Call to Holy Living: Section B—The Spirit and the Word." Pages 61–66 in *Growing to Maturity: A Messianic Jewish Discipleship Guide*. Clarksville: Messianic Jewish Publishers, 2011.

As seen from the above survey of governing documents and writings, the MJAA/IAMCS emphasizes the Spirit far more than Torah and tradition while the UMJC emphasizes Torah and tradition far more than the Spirit. It is not a matter of either/or but the relative weight of importance given to each area in their overall vision of Messianic Judaism.[18] Positively stated, these three major

---

18. The trajectories set by these three umbrella organizations are not always reflected among their members. There are MJAA/IAMCS congregations that are more tradition-oriented and UMJC congregations that are more Spirit-focused, e.g., UMJC synagogues and chavurah groups affiliated with Tikkun International. Tikkun's vision and values statement—"The Twelve Pillars: A Foundation for Tikkun Congregations & Ministries" (2018)—mentions the

xvii

Messianic Jewish organizations are complementary on the issue of the Spirit and Torah, and on a macro-level represent the broad spectrum. More negatively viewed, the Messianic Jewish community, as represented by the cross-section of the Alliance and the Union, has a major divide within it when it comes to its sense of priorities regarding the Spirit and Torah.[19]

And this brings us to the authors of this important work—Rabbi Joshua Lessard and Dr. Jen Rosner. While each presents their own perspective and there is no attempt to speak on behalf of others, the reality is that Joshua and Jen articulate views on the relationship between the Spirit and Torah that are largely in alignment with the thrust of the MJAA/IAMCS and UMJC positions respectively.[20] This is not surprising since Joshua is an IAMCS ordained rabbi and leads Tree of Life Messianic Fellowship, an IAMCS member congregation. By contrast, Jen is involved in UMJC circles. She is a protégé of Rabbi Mark Kinzer, a leading UMJC theologian, and

---

Spirit 55 times, the Torah 7 times, and tradition 2 times.

19. The Messianic Jewish community is not unique in grappling with the question of how to prioritize *both* the Spirit and Torah, "The relationship between the Spirit and the Word is an all-important one. Failure to realize this has accounted for many troubles in the long history of the Christian Church. People always tend to put the emphasis exclusively on one side or the other. The moment you separate the Spirit and the Word you are in trouble. There are some who say that having the illumination of the Spirit you do not need the Word at all. That was the tragedy of the Quakers. George Fox started with the right balance, but as he went on he increasingly tended to pay less and less attention to the Word and more and more to the 'inner light,' the illumination of the Spirit, the message received immediately . . . But then there is the other tendency, at the other extreme, to discount the Spirit, and to say that as long as we have the open Bible and the Word before us, and as long as we know it in some mechanical sense, we need nothing further. So the Spirit is forgotten, and you may have a dead orthodoxy, or a mere intellectual academic knowledge of the Scriptures, which really does not enable one to fight the battle against the devil and the principalities and the powers. The Spirit and the Word must be kept together always. The Spirit has provided for us the instruction found in the Word, but we cannot use it without Him. It can be a dead letter to us; 'the letter killeth, but the Spirit giveth life.' What is needed is the Spirit opening the Word, and opening my mind and opening my heart" (Lloyd-Jones, *Christian Soldier*, 328–29).

20. A notable exception to this simplism is Jen's focus on the significance of the Spirit in Messianic Judaism. See Rosner, "Witnesses."

FOREWORD

for a number of years was a member of a UMJC congregation in Los Angeles. While neither author represents the Alliance or Union in this correspondence, what the reader receives is a significant engagement with both communal perspectives on the Spirit and Torah from next-generation leaders who are affiliated in various ways with these two wings of the Messianic Jewish movement.

The dialogue in this book also models healthy theological discussion.[21] Joshua and Jen are thinking together and learning from each other with each letter written and reflected on. There is a refreshing respect for the power of words in the debate and how words can both hurt and heal.[22] As Rabbi Joseph Telushkin puts it:

> In a dispute with someone, you have the right to state your case, express your opinion, explain why you think the other party is wrong, even make clear how passionately you feel about the subject at hand. But these are the only rights you have. You do not have a moral right to undercut your adversary's position by invalidating him or her personally.[23]

In this correspondence, it is clear that each side is listening to the other before responding. Since Joshua and Jen genuinely want to understand each other's position, and not simply assume, they ask questions for clarification. There is a humility that comes through. They realize that, like the rest of us, they are on the learning curve.

There are a number of ways that we can more actively enter into the conversation between Joshua and Jen and get the most out of it. Here are several tips:

1. *We can adopt a holistic approach to truth.* A holistic approach avoids a one-sided perspective and concerns itself with the whole, including limitations and factors that affect implementation. As Klyne Snodgrass writes in his book *Between Two Truths*, "Truth is like a flower with deep roots. To enjoy it very long, we must take it all. If we take only the top part, it will

---

21. See Rudolph, "Guidelines"; Rudolph, "Reminder."
22. Prov 12:18; 18:21; *Lev. Rab.* 33.
23. Telushkin, *Words*, 89.

wither in our hands... Holistic thinking will cause us to look for tensions. When we know that a statement is true, we ought to ask what its limitations are, what other statements need to be made to prevent misunderstanding or extremism, and how circumstances might affect the implementation of the statement."[24]

2. *We can choose not to rehearse old thoughts and feelings.* Thinking together with our authors involves thinking and not simply rehearsing what we have long believed. In his book *Dialogue and the Art of Thinking Together*, William Isaacs writes, "What is true thinking? To think truly is to say things that may surprise us—things we have not said before—that are not in our memory... To think is also to listen to our own automatic reactions and gain perspective on them. It is to ask, Now, why did I do that?... What we usually call thinking is often merely the reporting or acting out of patterns already in our memory. Like a prerecorded tape, these thoughts (and feelings) are instantly ready for playback... True thinking moves more slowly, more gently than this... Thinking has a freshness to it, like a flow of water softly moving through the mind, and requires space. The fruit of thinking is sometimes a seemingly simple, quiet idea that stands out among a crowd of passing thoughts. It arrives unannounced."[25] Here is a good question to ask when wading through this book: How much of our "thinking" is coming from memory and is an automatic response? How much is based on original thinking about what we are reading?[26]

3. *We can follow the disturbance.* When our listening is colored by a disturbance (perhaps something Joshua or Jen has said that rubs us the wrong way), it is helpful to follow the disturbance and ask why we are bothered. This often leads to true thinking and new insights. By considering the source of the disturbance—whether it is in us, from them, or both—and

24. Snodgrass, *Between*, 180–84. See Rudolph, "Guidelines," 11.
25. Isaacs, *Dialogue*, 59–60.
26. See Rudolph, "Guidelines," 12.

why it irritates us, we become more keenly aware of what the person is actually saying. We may also recognize a tendency in us to respond to the disturbance by listening in a selective way—we may find ourselves instinctively sifting what they have said for evidence that we are right and they are wrong. Sometimes reframing helps. We can choose to see the person who disturbs us—Joshua or Jen—as a protector of important values within the Messianic Jewish movement rather than a nuisance. Following the disturbance may lead us to see our own inconsistency—we may realize that we have the same problem as the person whose words disturb us.[27]

Thinking together with Joshua and Jen about the relationship between the Spirit and Torah in Messianic Judaism moves us closer to the *achdut ha-emunah* ("unity of the faith") that Paul talks about in Ephesians 4:13. I believe that the next generation of Messianic Jews and Messianic Gentiles will overcome the divide that presently exists between the MJAA/IAMCS and UMJC, and that this will result in the presence and power of the Spirit being experienced in the Messianic Jewish community in ways that we have never seen before. Joshua and Jen are, in a sense, priming the pump of a broader dialogue that needs to take place in the Messianic movement in order that we might see this unity realized.

As readers, we are invited to consider who has the more compelling case in the correspondence. In this regard, we are not only evaluating which position is more in alignment with Scripture, our final authority for faith and practice, but also which perspective actually works (or works best) on the ground, in real life, and not just in an ivory tower. What does each trajectory lead to when applied to the local Messianic synagogue, the home, and one's personal walk with the Lord? Is one view more Pollyannaish than the other? Is there a way to bring them together? If we think only in the abstract, we can never answer these questions. We must get more specific.

One way to get more concrete is to apply the two approaches to individual commandments of God in the Scriptures and ask what the end results might look like, both practically and ethically. In this

---

27. See Rudolph, "Guidelines," 13.

vein, I recommend either reading through the Torah while contemplating the two perspectives put forward in this dialogue or reading the two-volume set *The Law of Messiah: Torah from a New Covenant Perspective* (Tikkun International, 2019) as a next step after reading Joshua and Jen's book. This is because the authors—Rabbi Michael Rudolph (my father) and Rabbi Daniel Juster—maintain an approach to the Spirit and Torah that on the spectrum is somewhere between Joshua and Jen, and they apply this *modus vivendi* to each of the *taryag mitzvot* (613 commandments).[28]

When reading Joshua and Jen's back-and-forth, it is important to keep in mind that the Torah itself is inspired by the Holy Spirit (2 Tim 3:16–17; 2 Pet 1:20–21) and has more than one purpose. There are at least twenty purposes of the Torah. They include:

1. To serve as the foundational revelation of God
2. To remind us of God's love, grace and power
3. To teach us how to love God and our neighbor
4. To teach us how to worship God
5. To establish the oneness and sovereignty of God
6. To teach us to be holy as God is holy
7. To point out sin so that we might return to God
8. To train us to exercise faith in God
9. To train us to be obedient to God
10. To reveal the heart and priorities of God
11. To reveal the wisdom and knowledge of God
12. To uphold the order of God's creation
13. To uphold God's standards of compassion and justice

---

28. "The resurgence of Jewish belief in Messiah Yeshua in the Twentieth Century has created a need for a fresh look at God's law applied with New Covenant principles and the Holy Spirit's interpretation, taking into account historic Rabbinic interpretations as well. This book seeks to fulfill that need by codifying and commenting on God's *mitzvot* wherever they may be found in Scripture—in the *Torah*, the *Nev'im*, the *Ketuvim*, the *Besorah* (Gospels) or the Apostolic Writings" (Rudolph with Juster, *Law,* 11).

14. To draw the nations to God
15. To foster unity among God's people
16. To give our children a heritage from the Lord
17. To demarcate Israel as a distinct and enduring nation by God's design
18. To prepare God's people for priestly service
19. To point us to Yeshua the Messiah
20. To train us to hear the voice of God

The Torah serves all of these purposes. Moreover, from the beginning, God intended Israel to observe his Torah with a heart turned toward him (Deut 6:5; 11:18; 26:16; 30:6, 14).

An area largely bracketed off in Joshua and Jen's discussion is the question of how Gentile believers in particular are supposed to relate to the Spirit and Torah today. This is a subject that requires extensive discussion and thus it is understandable that the authors felt it was beyond the scope of their correspondence. Nevertheless, since many of the readers of this book will be Gentiles in the Messianic movement and the wider body of Messiah, I would like to share several thoughts on this that are informed by having been part of the Messianic Jewish community for over 45 years and having reflected on this biblical-theological question for more than 30 years as a Messianic rabbi.

To begin with, while the Scriptures do not provide a list of *mitzvot* that are applicable to Gentiles, it is the historic view of the Jewish community, including the Messianic Jewish community, that God does not expect Gentiles to be circumcised or to observe Israel's festivals, among other distinctly Jewish commandments.[29]

---

29. For a Messianic Jewish response to the Hebrew Roots movement, see IAMCS, "One Law, Two Sticks" and Juster and Resnik, "One Law." Some groups, like First Fruits of Zion (FFOZ), argue on the basis of Zech 14 and other texts that everyone in the age to come will observe Israel's festivals and thus the biblical ideal is for all Gentile believers to observe them today. There are several problems with this argument: (1) It overstates what the Scriptures actually say. Zech 14 may refer to representatives of the nations going up to Jerusalem to celebrate *Sukkot* (the Feast of Tabernacles) and not everyone in the

This has been the majority view within Judaism for centuries. Moreover, this approach is consistent with the Jerusalem Council decision in Acts 15 (cf. 21:25) and Paul's "rule in all the congregations" (1 Cor 7:17–24).

What about Gentile believers who sense that God is calling them to worship in Jewish ways? The MJAA/IAMCS and UMJC affirm non-Jews who are called to join Messianic synagogues. "Called" is the operative word since the overwhelming majority of Gentile believers do not sense a calling in this direction. Stated another way, the MJAA/IAMCS and UMJC are in agreement that while the Gentile wing of the church should appreciate its Jewish origins, its Jewish Scriptures, and its Jewish Messiah, Gentile believers are not deficient in their faith if they do not follow distinctly Jewish customs.

There is a difference between calling and commandment. Gentile believers should view universal Torah ethics as divine imperatives to be observed in the power of the Spirit. It is a commandment to worship the Lord alone. It is a commandment not to commit adultery. It is a commandment to love one's neighbor as oneself. In contrast to these universal Torah ethics, more characteristically Jewish customs are matters of personal calling for Gentile followers of Yeshua. If a Gentile believer is drawn to live out some of these more Jewish-specific areas, this should derive from their being led by the Spirit and not from a sense of covenantal responsibility, which is unique to the Jewish people. Also, the individual should view the practice as something the Lord has called *them* to

---

world. Other annual festivals are not mentioned; (2) Even if God calls the nations to observe *Sukkot* and other aspects of Israel's calendar in the future, why would that mean Gentile believers should celebrate Jewish festivals today? Are we supposed to do everything now that will be done in the eschaton? Where do we see this principle in the Bible? Consider Yeshua's teaching, "For in the resurrection they neither marry nor are given in marriage, but are like angels in heaven" (Matt 22:30). Should God's people, therefore, not marry in the present age? Behind FFOZ's view is an over-realized eschatology; and (3) The consensus of New Testament scholarship is that Paul did not instruct Gentile believers to keep Israel's festivals. See Paul's pastoral guidance in Rom 14:5–6. In 1 Cor 5:8, he writes, "Therefore, let us celebrate the festival," but the context suggests that he is talking about living out the spiritual meaning of Passover.

FOREWORD

do and not something that God expects all Gentiles in the world to do (see Rom 14:5–6).[30]

At The King's University, where I serve as director of the Messianic Jewish Studies (MJS) program, we have Jewish and Gentile students, MJAA/IAMCS and UMJC students, as well as students from Christian churches and mainstream synagogues. Dr. Jack Hayford founded the university to be a Spirit-empowered institution of higher learning.[31] At the same time, the university is an approved school of the UMJC for rabbinical ordination and *madrikh* (teacher) certification training, hence there is a commitment to the importance of Torah and tradition in Messianic Jewish life. This explains why we have a Torah scroll displayed by the front entrance, one of the first things that someone sees when entering the school. This coming together of Spirit and Torah in the DNA of our university has meant that faculty members teach about the relationship between the Spirit and Torah to our students. Sometimes it is unpacked along the lines of Joshua and Jen's book, and other times it is broken down into something more simple so that students don't miss the forest for the trees.

When I teach "Messianic Jewish Theology" and want to bring my students back to the bigger picture of how the Spirit and Torah fit into the overall priorities of God's kingdom, I present Rabbi Juster's FYSTR model, which helps to strike the balance in a Messianic Jewish context. Rabbi Juster writes:

> Messianic Judaism is New Covenant Judaism and Messianic Jewish theology must emphasize the benefits and realities of New Covenant life. This does not mean that we do not give the Torah and the Prophets their full due. However, the issue is one of emphasis...
>
> The Bible exhorts us to give honor to whom honor is due (Rom 13:7). Those who have given us the post-biblical Jewish heritage are to be honored for all that is good, true and beautiful in the heritage of our people. Most cultures

---

30. Given concerns about covenant-related traditions and cultural appropriation, it is wisdom to walk this out with sensitivity to Jewish community norms and in consultation with a Messianic rabbi or pastor.

31. See Hayford, *Living*; Rudolph, "Count Zinzendorf."

have honorable traditions and practices due to the grace of God given to all people. For us as Jews, the Jewish heritage comes from our ancestral fathers and out of our covenantal relationship before God as his people... Our view of the Rabbinic heritage is that *we must be discerning; approving what is good and rejecting that which is not good or not in accord with the letter and the spirit of the Bible.* In addition, our adoption of any tradition even if it is good, when it is not commanded in the Bible, is to be embraced when we are so led by the Spirit; there is to be no rule beyond that. Only a person who has a renewed mind—with their heart priorities in order—can rightly evaluate, since evaluation is a function of the whole person.

I have traveled to many countries and pleaded in my teaching that we must all understand the centrality of Yeshua and the power of the Spirit as primary. If this is not established, we will not be able to evaluate with mature judgment. Yeshua is to be *explicitly* central and pervasive in our preaching and our worship. In John 5, Yeshua declares that the Father desires that we honor the Son as we honor him. Only then can we have God's powerful Presence among us. If we do not do this, we will not have his powerful Presence. We must teach people to seek the presence of the Spirit and to appropriate his power, without which we cannot accomplish God's works of love and service.

In teaching this, I have written an acrostic: FYSTR. The acrostic represents the relative emphases that we should seek. The New Covenant Scriptures provide us with these emphases. First we emphasize the Father and Yeshua in our worship and preaching. This is in accord with the consistent devotional expression in the New Covenant Scriptures and the consistent and pervasive affirmation that Yeshua is fully deity and fully man. Then we emphasize the Spirit, without whom we do not have the power of obedience or the ability to extend God's kingdom. The gifts and power of the Spirit are critical. Then there is the Torah—the teaching of God's ways—the very commandments themselves. Finally there is the Rabbinic heritage,

FOREWORD

which has its proper place but only in accordance with the relative emphasis of the acrostic. We could add that the post-biblical Christian understanding is also a source of wisdom, provided always that it too does not contradict Scripture. We think that if we keep this proper order, we will see a strong and vibrant Jewish expression of our faith.[32]

The FYSTR model is intended to be simple and can serve as a starting point for evaluating other models, including the ones encountered in this book.

I felt a special joy reading Joshua and Jen's work for the first time because both of them are affiliated with The King's University—Joshua as a graduate student in Messianic Jewish studies and Jen as a faculty member who teaches Messianic Jewish Theology among other MJS courses online. Together, they represent well the vision of our program and the hope of the MJAA/IAMCS/UMJC to bring the Spirit and Torah together in Messianic Judaism. Their dialogue advances this goal since it will help many in the Messianic Jewish world to think more deeply about these questions, and to deliberate in a way that is collaborative, generous and Spirit-led, as Joshua and Jen have done so beautifully.

DAVID RUDOLPH, PHD
Director of Messianic Jewish Studies
The King's University

---

32. Juster, "Lecture 6–2," 1, 4.

INTRODUCTION

I have to admit, when I found out my brother was engaged, I was quite happy for him. When I found out he was marrying Jennifer Rosner, one of the top young scholars in the Messianic Jewish movement, I was happy for myself. Now a new voice could be added to our family discussions of God, the Bible, and the nature of Jewish practice for Messianic Jews. These were discussions I always thrived on and, while attempting, sometimes successfully, not to be overbearing, I often tried to find ways of turning many of our conversations towards issues of faith and spiritual practice. Sometimes I was driven by the mere intellectual challenge of engaging with others; in the purer moments, the conversations were driven by a love for God and a curiosity to see what new spiritual discoveries could be made through our discourses. Jen has proven to be a wonderful wife for my brother, a devoted mother for their children, and a worthy interlocutor in our family discussions.

Not too many years after she married my brother, I took her Messianic Jewish Theology course at The King's University. The course was as I expected: organized, thorough, and profound. During the course, however, I noticed our approach towards certain topics to be at variance. I wasn't terribly surprised by this given our previous discussions, but the depth of our differences on certain matters was becoming more obvious. The paper I wrote for that class focused on aspects of Paul's approach to Torah and prompted an email conversation between us. Early on in that discussion, it was obvious to me that we each represented various streams within Messianic Judaism that were vying and continue to vie for the upper hand in defining our movement as we move into the future. I thought it would be beneficial to take that email conversation to a more presentable format and consider, should we find the end result worthy, publishing it. The book that follows is that conversation. The purpose of presenting it to the wider public is to give those on each side, and the few who remain undecided, food for thought. While there are already sophisticated voices for both sides, the tendency is often to read and listen to those voices with whom one already agrees. This book, we hope, will encourage a thoughtful reflection of both sides.[1]

Messianic Judaism's relationship to Torah is a topic that Jen and I have both thought about, studied, and prayed over long and hard. I am sure there is truth in both of our presentations. However, the gap between our approaches is wide enough that the law of noncontradiction must apply. While there are ways to take a piecemeal approach and apply my viewpoint in one context and Jen's in another, that we are seeking to sway the general direction for an entire movement means that at least one of us is wrong. Neither of us is wrong in everything, and there are many things about which we do agree—foundational, important things. Nevertheless, were those who agree with my line of thinking to have the upper hand in guiding the movement, it would look, I believe, far different and be focused on different concerns than if those in Jen's camp were to guide the movement. That means that this is a vitally important topic for those in the Messianic Jewish movement. In addition, I think it should be a matter of great interest for Christian readers who must assess their own relationship with the growing Messianic Jewish movement and with the first five books of their Bible. Christians may also find that our dialogue mirrors, to a large extent, their own grapplings with the relationship between tradition and Spirit. I believe that Jewish readers who are not Messianic may also find this conversation of interest as they discover parallels in Jen's or my thinking with issues of Torah, freedom, and peoplehood. This is a topic about which Messianic Jews in particular *should* be reading and prayerfully contemplating the perspectives of those with whom they do and do not agree.

---

1. We are not unaware that there are more than two sides in this debate. We are representing our personal views which happen to align relatively well with two of the primary approaches to Messianic Jewish expression.

INTRODUCTION

Within this conversation I consider myself a voice for the Messianic movement as it was understood during its American resurgence in the 1960s and 70s. Granted that I wasn't born until 1974, I think I have a fair understanding of that time period having grown up in the Messianic movement, conversed with some of those who were in the movement from the start, and read historical and theological books that discussed those early days. Surely the nascent movement did not come out of the birth canal fully developed. Theological maturation was a necessity in the face of new and challenging questions. How does a Messianic movement remain Jewish in the face of so many Gentiles joining? Who is a Jew? How traditional should our services be? What is our place in relation to the rest of the body of Messiah? What is the place of Torah in our individual and corporate lives? What place should the charismatic gifts have in our corporate worship? Notwithstanding this lack of consensus, what was understood by that first generation was that Messianic Judaism was a work of God. It was a revivalist movement that thrived on a non-coerced, natural (if somewhat limited) Jewish expression and an emphasis on the supernatural in both outreach and congregational worship. However else our theology and practice may develop, it is this revivalist spirit of Messianic Judaism that I feel called to defend.

Growing up, my family and I belonged to a congregation that was one of the charter members of the Union of Messianic Jewish Congregations (UMJC). This may have been the first congregational organization for Messianic Judaism in history. Beginning in the late 1990s, new voices associated with the movement arose. These voices were represented by groups such as *Hashivenu* and the Messianic Jewish Rabbinical Council. The claim of these groups is that our theological maturity and stability as a truly Jewish movement must be found within a closer relationship to normative, religious Judaism; that is, Rabbinic Judaism. Dr. Rosner's is a compelling voice within this current of Messianic Jewish thought.

From my perspective, the questions that we must ask in assessing this call to a more Orthodox Jewish approach are these: 1) Should Messianic Judaism continue to be defined as a revivalist movement, and if so, 2) is a focus on adhering to rabbinic thought and standards compatible with this definition? In this book I express my concerns in regard to Rabbinic Judaism's compatibility with a Spirit-led movement while Jen expresses her thoughts on our inability to be the Jewish movement God has called us to be apart from it.

Perhaps we could add one more question to the mix. Should we not come to a consensus on one or both of the questions above, can we move forward peacefully as a single movement? My sincere hope is that we can. Perhaps in addition to informing our readers about our differences, this book presents a larger narrative that is implicit in the very format and tone in which it is presented. This larger narrative declares that unity is possible in the midst of diversity and that love need not be lessened by differences, that the other side deserves the honor of a listening ear and a respectful response because, in the end, more than we are opponents, we are brothers and sisters in Yeshua who are compelled to action by God's continuing faithfulness to Israel and the world. I believe fully in what I present in this book just as Jen believes fully in what she has presented. We each also believe that this is an important topic that must be honestly and openly discussed. The discussion herein is respectful in tone, but also painfully honest and, at times, quite personal. My hope is that the fact that Jen and I are literally family can serve as a symbol for our movement as we grapple to find our way without losing our brothers and sisters.

In Messiah's love,
Joshua Lessard

OCTOBER 17, 2018

Dear Jen,

I want to thank you for your instruction, your insight, and your commitment to the maturing of the Messianic Jewish movement. Based on earlier conversations, I can say that there is much on which we agree. Among other things, we both hold to the authority of the Tanakh (Hebrew Bible) and the B'rit Chadashah (New Testament), we both maintain a very high Christology, and we both believe that Israel has an ongoing and positive role in the plan of God for the earth.

There are also areas of respectful disagreement and the purpose of this correspondence is to discuss these differences. I am entering this discussion for three reasons: 1) It gives me a voice to speak to you, someone I respect and believe will continue to have an influence on a growing segment of our movement, about things that I feel are of the utmost importance. I hope to sway you, at least in part, toward my side of the issues at hand. This does not mean that I see anything wrong with your life or lifestyle. I am in no position to judge your relationship with God, and the fruit I have seen in your life unquestionably reveals the love of God. Nonetheless, I believe that what I will present in this correspondence can produce positive fruit in our movement, so I try to sway as many as possible towards that end; 2) I hope to be taught by you. I genuinely want to know where my own ideas might be weak and where my presentation can be honed to express greater truth; 3) In answering your questions and challenges, I fully expect that I will need to dig deeply into the Scriptures and wrestle with God in my prayer life. I expect this to be a challenging and rewarding journey.

So to begin, I will present where I think a great part of our disagreement lies. I believe that we disagree over the nature and focus of Torah observance for modern Messianic Jews. I will pose my general thoughts on Torah (here at least, defined as the five books of Moses and the general approach towards obedience that those books engender) and our relationship to it. I eagerly await your reply.

Paul states the following in Galatians 5:18: "But if you are led by the *Ruach*, you are not under Law."[1] Paul's use of *nomos* (law) here is without the article and shows that being "under law" is describing a general approach to life in which evil tendencies are constrained by laws (be they Roman, Jewish, or whatever). While *nomos* here does not only refer to Torah, it does include Torah when it is approached as a law code. What Paul's proposal of being led by the Spirit means in relation to Torah is that Torah, while remaining vital for gaining wisdom and insight into the righteousness and glory of God (among other things), no longer contains an in force law code. That is, we are not hemmed in by rules and regulations to guard us against our natural proclivities for unrighteousness, but rather, the Spirit within us transforms us so that we naturally bring forth the fruits of righteousness. Within this mindset, laws become a type of helpful check on our relationship with God. For example, even though I may not feel compelled to tithe because the commandment to do so no longer has the force of law, I ought nevertheless to engage with that law and realize that there is a spiritual issue (rather than a legal issue) if I am not generous with my finances. I use the law as a corrective in the way it reveals the heart of God in my following of the Spirit.

The Torah itself was never simply a matter of obeying rules; it elevates love (Deut 6:4–5) and a circumcised heart (Deut 10:16). Nonetheless, the very nature of much of the Torah reveals that the love and circumcision of heart for which Israel should have strived would be incomplete at best. Moses' prophecy of the falling away of Israel (Deut 4:25; 31:24–29) revealed the inadequacy of the Torah to truly make the people wholehearted to the Lord. This sentiment is echoed in Jeremiah 31:31(32)[2] and Romans 8:3. In fact, a large

---

1. All Scripture passages from the Tree of Life (TLV) Version of the Bible. Copyright © 2015 by The Messianic Jewish Family Bible Society.

2. Verses in parentheses are given when Christian verse numbering differs

percentage of the Torah is specifically geared towards a wayward people (as any people not reborn of the Spirit would have been) and, because of this, contains a plethora of rules, regulations, and promises of blessings and curses. All of this was meant to preserve some sense of holiness so that God might dwell in Israel's midst and preserve them as a people for his own good purposes.

Therefore, when Paul says that those who are in the Spirit are not "under law," or when he says that "the *Torah* is not given for a *tzaddik* [righteous person] but for the lawless and rebellious" (1 Tim 1:9a) he is obviously not dismissing Torah as a continuing source of wisdom (2 Tim 3:16), nor has it been demoted from its position as Scripture. Indeed, he defends Yeshua as the Messiah because the Torah and the prophets point to him (Rom 3:21). However, Torah as law used to keep a rebellious people in check has been replaced by a life transformed by the indwelling of the Spirit and bearing the fruit and gifts of the Spirit. Life in the Spirit will fulfill all of the major intents of Torah (love, circumcision of heart, etc.), but it may or may not overlap with the specific commandments of Torah.

Furthermore, I contend that such a life in the Spirit is inconsistent with following rabbinic thought and practice as the climax of our spiritual expression. I find nothing wrong with lighting Shabbat candles, praying from a *siddur*, avoiding eating milk and meat together, etc. However, these things are only beneficial for those who are called to do so according to the Spirit. It would not surprise me were most, if not all, Messianic Jews called to interact with Rabbinic Judaism on some level, even if I would venture that for many Messianic Jews that level would be fairly minimal. However, even those who are called to interact deeply with rabbinic practice must not see Jewish orthodoxy as the height of their religious devotion, for even in its purest expression rabbinism is a continuation of the Mosaic Torah as given to our wayward ancestors. Rabbinic Judaism rightly emphasizes the mercy of God, pure devotion to God, *kavannah*, etc. However, its texts are filled with rule after rule and thus reveal that a circumcised heart in which one naturally does what

---

from those in Jewish Bibles.

is right is not really expected. In Paul's division of being led by the Spirit or being under law, the practical results of the approach of Rabbinic Judaism (regardless of its intent) is to keep people more concerned with law than being led by the Spirit.

To give an analogy: a classroom with rebellious children needs a lot of rules and a lot of the consequences (good and bad) spelled out. A classroom full of children with a heart to learn and respect others may not need any rules; these children automatically do what is conducive to their heart's desire to learn and love. Their own hearts rule them. We are called to be like that second classroom. Perhaps this is what Paul meant when he said we were no longer under the Torah as our *paidagogos* (Gal 3:24–25). An overemphasis on rules contradicts the fact that our born-again lives are not in need of such minutia. Even those specifically called to such an observant life must not confuse the rules themselves with righteousness, but rather understand that righteousness is in following the Spirit which, in their individual case, would include the minutiae of strict Torah observance.

The results of my understanding of Torah in the age of the poured-out Spirit would mean that the five books of Moses are revered as Scripture and seen as a source of godly wisdom and a prophetic voice that set the stage for Messiah. We should interact with the Torah by the Spirit, allowing the Spirit to bring out the aim of the laws, teachings, and narratives. At times we will apply the commandments literally; at all times the commandments will remind us of the heart we should possess by revealing God's heart. This approach will result in an emphasis on the major principles above the literal application. Rabbinic writings can also be gleaned for wisdom, and varying amounts of rabbinic practices can be incorporated for the sake of those things that are in line with how God may be leading individuals or local communities. However, according to my understanding, an overriding theology which upholds the Torah as a current law code, and especially one that adds to it the idea of the rabbis as authoritative interpreters of Torah for Messianic Jews, would be rejected. The ideal for which we should strive is not to be people in need of an overreaching law system

OCTOBER 17, 2018

(including that system presented in Torah and rabbinism), but to be those who are transformed and led by the Spirit.

I look forward to your reply.

Shalom,
Josh

OCTOBER 24, 2018

Dear Josh,

Thank you for starting this correspondence, and I too look forward to the opportunity to be sharpened and challenged by our dialogue. Let me begin with a few responses to your initial explanation:

1. To develop further what you've already explained, it seems that the heart of our disagreement is how the coming of Messiah and the giving of the Spirit changes the meaning of Torah and what our practices and actions should look like as a result. We both agree that *something* has changed; the nature and definition of that change is the catalyst for this discussion.

2. You state that "a large percentage of the Torah is specifically geared toward a wayward people (as any people not reborn of the Spirit would have been)." You seem to draw a sharp distinction here between the biblical people of Israel as "wayward," and a people reborn of the Spirit as correlatively *not* wayward. I would disagree. From the perspective of theological anthropology, I don't think humanity has fundamentally changed after the coming of Messiah and the giving of the Spirit. Therefore, I disagree with the assertion that the "minutiae" of the Torah are no longer required because Spirit-led human beings are no longer wayward. From my perspective, humanity (whether Spirit-led or not) is every bit as wayward as it has always been. This doesn't mean that the Spirit didn't change something, but the fundamental waywardness of the human heart is, in my opinion, *not* what changed.

3. Along these lines, I find a problem with your classroom analogy. Granted, there are certainly children that may be more or

October 24, 2018

less rebellious—and more or less eager to learn and please—than other children. However, they are all still *children*. They will all, on occasion, be distracted, disobedient, inclined toward competitive and unfriendly conduct, etc. To claim that "a classroom full of children with a heart to learn and respect others may not need any rules" is naive, from my perspective. All children need guidance, direction and boundaries. To the extent that we are these children (per your analogy), so do we.

4. To apply the above analogy to the Torah, there is an aspect of your position that seems to be an argument from silence. I come to the New Testament with the belief that Yeshua's Jewish followers fully maintained a life of Torah, though there was adamant debate about what was required of *Gentile* followers of Yeshua (see, for example, Acts 15). Paul declares himself to be a Pharisee (present tense, Acts 23:6). If the New Testament were advocating for a radical departure from Torah observance as widely understood in the world of Second Temple Judaism, I think this would be much more explicit. While some of the passages you mention may seem to hint in this direction (i.e., Gal 5:18), I believe that a close read of the context of these passages reveals a different story. The first few verses of Galatians 5 make it quite clear that Paul is speaking to Gentiles here; he is strongly advising them *not* to be circumcised. I believe he would never say this to a Jewish audience (see Acts 16:3, where Paul himself circumcises Timothy).

Now, a few questions for you based upon what you have written:

1. While we agree that *something* changed with the coming of Messiah and the giving of the Spirit (not least with regard to what Torah means), I don't understand exactly how you are categorizing this change. In other words, what is the relationship between a life following Torah and a life following the Spirit? I have in mind a Venn diagram—if the Torah is one circle and the Spirit is another circle, what determines the extent to which they overlap? Is it possible that they wouldn't overlap at all (i.e., is it possible that the Spirit would lead one

to disregard explicit commandments in the Torah)? While I appreciate the biblical emphasis placed on the freedom of the Spirit, I do question whether the Spirit would lead in a way that directly opposes the Torah.

2. Also, I'm not sure if we see eye to eye on the ongoing significance of Jew/Gentile distinction. While I agree that a certain approach to this topic can lead to division and hierarchy, I think that proper implementation of this distinction avoids both and follows the example of Scripture. In this regard, I also see Torah as a unique heritage of the Jewish people, and the loss of Torah as a way of life has led to the loss of distinction of the Jewish people (assimilation). This adds another layer of significance to actual Torah observance and not some spiritualized version of it.

3. Finally, I think the very definition of Torah may be at issue here. Every branch of Judaism has their own history of interpretation and halakhic guidelines for how to implement the precepts of the Torah. And I believe that each branch would still call it Torah. So, would it be fair to say that you are attempting to outline what a uniquely Messianic Jewish approach to Torah is (or should be) as opposed to claiming that the New Testament in some way abrogates Torah?

4. You state that "even those who are called to interact deeply with rabbinic practice must not see rabbinic expression as the height of their religious devotion, for in its purest form rabbinism is a continuation of the Mosaic Torah as given to our wayward ancestors." I think this statement reveals a deep difference in how each of us perceives rabbinic tradition (and, perhaps correlatively, Christian tradition). It seems premature to tackle this topic at this point, though I think it needs to be addressed and wrestled through as we continue our discussion.

I look forward to your reply,
Jen

OCTOBER 29, 2018

Dear Jen,

I appreciate your thoughts and questions. The thought that jumped out at me as showing the greatest distance between us was in your second point. You wrote: "From my perspective, humanity (whether Spirit-led or not) is every bit as wayward as it has always been." I agree that even after the outpouring of the Holy Spirit in Acts 2, humanity in general is no less wayward. I would even agree that many of those who claim to be followers of Yeshua have at times exhibited a waywardness that was as extreme or worse than Israel when they were denounced by the prophets. However, I have to take a rather strong exception to your inclusion of Spirit-led people in with a humanity that is "every bit as wayward as it has always been." I'm not proposing that Spirit-led people, myself included, are perfect, but I see being Spirit-led and being wayward as so diametrically opposed that I don't understand how someone can be both at the same time. In fact, when I am wayward, it's precisely because I'm not being Spirit-led at the moment.

It was the very power of the Spirit to bring transformation that caused Paul to set following the Spirit as a higher mode of living than the constant struggle to do right under the Torah (Rom 7, 8). This is in line with the prophets who foretold that the coming answer to waywardness would not be a rabbinic class that would "make a fence around the Torah" but the outpouring of the Spirit (Ezek 36, 37; Isa 44:3).

It seems clear to me that the connection with water and the coming outpouring of the Spirit in Ezekiel 36:25–26 and Isaiah 44:3 is what Yeshua is building upon in John 3:5 (understanding "water" and "spirit" as a hendiadys),[1] 4:14, and 7:38. The fulfillment of these

---

1. Carson, *The Gospel*, 191.

Holy Spirit promises awaited Yeshua's glorification. "Now He said this about the *Ruach*, whom those who trusted in Him were going to receive; for the *Ruach* was not yet given, since *Yeshua* was not yet glorified" (John 7:39). Yeshua's glorification took place when He ascended to the Father (John 17:5). So if the Spirit is the healing of our waywardness according to the prophets, and if Yeshua delivers the Spirit at his glorification, then it follows that those who believe in him should be healed of their waywardness. The fact that only a remnant of Jews participated in this outpouring through faith in Yeshua, the fact that a larger Jewish revival awaits a later time, and the fact that it may only be a minority of those who claim to follow Yeshua who actually live according to this manner of spiritual existence, does not negate the eschatological reality that we are invited to take part in.

I think my response to your second point would apply to some extent to your third point. Immature children need rules. The mature who sometimes get off track need to be reminded of the larger picture. An immature student will be told that they broke rule "X" so the consequence is "Y" (and this is the nature of much of the Torah). The mature student will be told to remember the larger perspective of why they are in the classroom and to remember to be motivated toward the higher calling they have. I believe that the general thought here is backed up by Galatians 3 and 1 Timothy 1:8–11. That we still need rules (since those mature in following the Spirit share the classroom with those who are young in the Spirit or are not Spirit-led at all) is obvious. Equally obvious, I would argue, is that the New Testament's ideal is not to be motivated by the written rule but by the inner rule of the Spirit. The written rule may be to raise your hand before you speak. At the foundation of that written rule is the greater reality that order is the aim. The immature child will be taught to raise his hand at all times. The mature child will always aim for order which may or may not include raising her hand depending on the particular situation in the classroom. She will be attuned to the reality around her and will be led by her desire for order as to the appropriate response. Rules are still necessary, but they are not to be the emphasis of the life of a believer.

OCTOBER 29, 2018

Your question about a spiritualized version of the Torah can be answered here. The extensive list of blessings and curses at the end of Deuteronomy was a necessary motivating factor for those who had not been regenerated by the Spirit of God. But the new heart of which Ezekiel prophesied and Yeshua promised is no longer motivated by such things. In fact, the blessings of Yeshua in Matthew 5:3–10, for the most part, are of quite a different nature than the blessings of Deuteronomy. In Deuteronomy for example, our enemies are defeated before us (28:7). In Matthew we are blessed when we are persecuted. In Deuteronomy we are blessed with physical fertility (28:4–5). In Matthew, we are blessed with seeing God and being called a child of God. How do we go from desiring the blessings of defeating enemies and physical prosperity to the highly spiritual blessings of seeing God through being the mourners, the meek, and the persecuted? How do we go from feeling that defeat in battle means God's curse to being like Richard Wurmbrand who could see his chains in a Communist prison as musical instruments for the praise of God, or like the apostles who rejoiced at their persecution (Acts 5:41)?[2] There is only one answer: the transformation by the Spirit through faith in Yeshua. The written Torah is there to guide us and reveal the heart and wisdom of God, but we need a spiritual approach to Torah for a spiritually transformed people. We don't need a Torah telling us exactly how much to tithe and enforce it by law, but an approach that says, "Each one must give as he has decided in his heart, not reluctantly or under compulsion, for God loves a cheerful giver" (2 Cor 9:7).

You questioned whether I was attempting a Messianic Jewish approach to Torah. I am in fact not doing that here, rather I am offering a general approach for all believers in Yeshua, an approach in which the Torah guides and informs but does not rule. Messianic Jews (and Gentiles in our midst) may very well adhere to a closer connection with the laws through the guidance of the Spirit. Many of us, myself included, have our communal worship on the Sabbath, hold a Passover seder, avoid pork, etc. However, this general pursuit

---

2. I heard Richard Wurmbrand tell the story of using his chains for musical accompaniment in a speech he gave in the 1990s at Beth Messiah Synagogue of Tidewater.

of life in the Spirit versus being under Torah as a law code is an ideal for all believers. This, of course, leads to your concern about the "ongoing Jew/Gentile" distinction.

In the New Testament we find that the major dividing line is not between Jew and Gentile (as it was in the Tanakh) but between those who do and those who do not follow Yeshua as the light of the world. His life, death, resurrection, and his identity as the fully divine Messiah, are the revealed realities by which all other things are now judged. My Jewishness, or someone else's identity as a non-Jew, matters only to the extent that Yeshua is given glory. Therefore, the main concern is being in Messiah and Messiah being glorified through the testimony of individuals and communities who come to him and follow him. The Gentile testimony is important and testifies that the God of Israel is the God of all the earth. The Jewish testimony is likewise important and testifies concerning God's ongoing faithfulness to the promises he made to the patriarchs, David, and the prophets. We testify that God is faithful throughout all time.

I have no burden on me to preserve that testimony beyond what God through his Spirit and Word leads me to do. There are various ways he can lead so that a recognizable Jewish testimony is maintained. This can include choices in worship, eating, and participating in Jewish cultural events and expressions. It can include marrying a Jewish spouse or moving to Israel. It can also include varying degrees of literal Torah application. However, because the very nature of the testimony is the unique manner in which God has called and leads the individual to bring him glory, I cannot write a list of things that Jews and Gentiles should and should not do as long as each is living within the major precepts of the Bible and being led by the Spirit. Someone may say, for example, that Messianic Jews should marry other Messianic Jews to maintain our testimony as Jews. But perhaps God is calling a Messianic Jew to marry a believing Gentile as a sign of the "one new man" (Eph 2) or for the sake of reaching intermarried couples. Intermarriage, therefore, can also be a testimony, and testimony is the main goal. This does not mean that we participate in things which have no real meaning for us as an underhanded way of evangelism. Messiah is our life (John 14:6), so that which points to him is infused with deep meaning, and we take up the worship and life expressions that point to him with joy! Therefore, I would relegate the Jewish/Gentile distinction within the body of Messiah to an issue of testimony rather than substantive differences, and the manner in which this testimony is best maintained is through the guidance of individuals and local communities by the Holy Spirit. The New Testament emphasizes absolute unity between Jewish and Gentile believers in Yeshua (John 10:16; 17:20–21; Gal 3:28; Eph 2:11ff; 4:4–6); we must maintain this.

I believe that my understanding in this matter would relate back to your fourth point. You stated: "I come to the New Testament with the belief that Yeshua's Jewish followers fully maintained a life of Torah, though there was adamant debate about what was required of *Gentile* followers of Yeshua (see, for example, Acts 15)." I don't doubt that many of the first-generation Jewish believers did maintain a life of Torah. However, it is equally clear that Torah observance was not maintained as the highest spiritual expression of their faith. That is why when the Temple fell and large parts of Torah observance became impossible without radical re-interpretation, that faith was able to thrive. It is also why, in an age where the manner of Torah observance was hotly debated between various sects of Judaism, the New Testament contains no record of trying to sort out the proper manner of this observance. There were Hellenistic Jews and Hebraic Jews in the early congregation (Acts 6:1), and the concern was not that the Hellenists become Hebrews or maintain Hebrew Jewish standards, but that their widows not be neglected.[3]

You stated: "Paul declares himself to be a Pharisee (present tense, Acts 23:6)." We have no working definition that can firmly decipher the boundary lines of Pharisaism in the first century. In the context of Acts 23, we know Paul at least meant it in regard to

---

3. That the designations *Hellenist* and *Hebrew* should mean more than a linguistic background but also include a difference in levels of Torah observance, see Philippians 3:5 where Paul describes his former life as "a Hebrew of Hebrews" (also see 2 Cor. 11:22) as evidence that his qualifications as an observant Jew are not surpassed by his theological adversaries. Also see comments on Acts 6:1 in Longenecker, "Acts," 802.

his belief in the resurrection from the dead. It may also have meant that his general lifestyle could be characterized as Pharisaic. But it would be overreaching to say that his philosophy in regard to Torah was strictly Pharisaic by his use of this term in this situation in which resurrection of the dead, and not Torah observance, was the emphasis of his defense.

You said: "If the New Testament were advocating for a radical departure from Torah observance as widely understood in the world of Second Temple Judaism, I think this would be much more explicit. While some of the passages you mention may seem to hint in this direction (ex., Gal 5:18), I believe that a close read of the context of these passages reveals a different story. The first few verses of Galatians 5 make it quite clear that Paul is speaking to Gentiles here; he is strongly advising them *not* to be circumcised. I believe he would never say this to a Jewish audience (see Acts 16:3, where Paul himself circumcises Timothy)." The New Testament's point is not a "radical departure from Torah observance" but neither is it to radically observe Torah when defined as a law code. I would argue that Torah in the New Testament is indeed upheld, and even magnified, in its spiritual goals. The New Testament's point is that a newly revealed reality has eclipsed the issue of Torah observance altogether so that "neither circumcision counts for anything nor uncircumcision" (1 Cor 7:19). To advise Gentiles not to undergo circumcision makes this exact point: "Don't do it," Paul could be paraphrased as saying, "because it is not by Torah but rather by grace that you have a right standing with God." Likewise, to create a reactionary movement against Torah by Jewish believers would characterize them not as the people of the Jewish Messiah, but as the people against Torah. This would also make Torah the central issue, only in a negative fashion.

What is repeatedly revealed in the New Testament is that the highest goal of a believer's spiritual expression is not Torah observance, nor is it a concerted effort to avoid observing Torah, but rather following in the footsteps of Messiah's sacrificial love by way of the outpoured Spirit. We live in an age without a functioning Temple or priesthood. Torah observance, for the most part, has come to be defined by the mandates of rabbis who are not

Messianic. Most Messianic Jews live in communities where rabbinic Torah observance would be cumbersome and require major life changes. Due to these factors it seems to me that the time and effort it would take to attempt some form of exacting Torah observance would, for most, automatically result in a de-emphasis on the things of the Spirit, including the freedom of being led by the Spirit from within rather than a multitude of written laws from without. Paul contrasts life according to the Spirit with life under Torah in several places and maintains that life in the Spirit is superior. This superior life is not reserved for the non-Jew alone.

Looking forward to your reply.

Shalom,
Josh

NOVEMBER 4, 2018

Josh,

I would agree that we are now getting closer to the heart of our differences. With regard to humanity's waywardness, you seem to suggest that the Torah had no power to curb this quality whereas in contrast, the Spirit has indeed paved the way for an obedient and faithful people of God. While you thus juxtapose Spirit and Torah, I see them working in conjunction.

You cite Ezekiel 36 as a portrait of God's promise to give the people a new Spirit. However, according to Ezekiel, what is it that this outpouring of the Spirit will bring about? "I will put My *Ruach* within you. Then I will cause you to walk in My laws, so you will keep My rulings and do them" (Ezek 36:27). Here, the very purpose of the Spirit is to enable the people to properly abide by God's laws (Torah)! Rather than being a juxtaposition to the Torah, the Spirit will finally provide the opportunity for dedicated observance of Torah.

Of course, according to the New Testament, the Spirit is also the means by which Gentiles are able to glorify God alongside Jews. Allow me to quote extensively from a paper I have written on this topic:

> The vision of Torah observant Messianic Judaism hinges upon the divine empowerment brought by God's Spirit. While Messiah provides atonement for sins and models for us the perfect fulfillment of Torah, our baptism and reception of the gift of his Spirit enables us to boldly follow in his footsteps. By the power of the Spirit, Israel is thus empowered to faithfully live out the life to which it is called, a life of obedience and submission to God.
>
> Acts 3–9 includes numerous references to the Spirit's presence and power among the believers, and Acts

10 tells the story of the surprising inclusion of Gentiles in this ever-expanding movement of God. When Peter recounts the narrative of God's work in Messiah at Cornelius' house—after both Peter and Cornelius have received visions from God—"the Holy Spirit came on all who heard the message" (Acts 10:44). Peter and his Jewish companions "were astonished that the gift of the Holy Spirit had been poured out even on the Gentiles" (Acts 2:45). In this regard, the Spirit indeed extends the work of Messiah; God's presence and holiness continues to expand outward, astonishing even those Jews who had followed Yeshua and had been participating in his mission. Apparently they had not yet realized the full implications of the outward expansion of God's reign of which they themselves were a part.

The presence of the Spirit among both Jews and Gentiles illustrates what it actually means that the "wall of hostility" has been torn down. In Peter's vision in Acts 10, he is instructed "not to call impure anything that God has made clean" (Acts 10:15). Peter's understanding of this vision has everything to do with fellowship between Jews and Gentiles, as evidenced by the interpretation he offers in Acts 11 and Acts 15. In Acts 11, the response of the "circumcised believers" to Peter's explanation is: "So then, God has granted even the Gentiles repentance unto life" (Acts 11:18).

Indeed, it is precisely the gift of the Spirit that identifies and concretizes unity and fellowship between Jews and Gentiles. Three times in the book of Acts, it is noted that the Spirit came upon the Gentiles *just as he came upon the Jews* (Acts 10:47, 11:15, 15:8–9). This, for the Jewish believers, was the overwhelming proof that God's work extended beyond the people of Israel.

However, it was determined early on that the *implications* of the gift of the Spirit—and of God's presence and work—are not the same for Jews as for Gentiles. This is the issue that occasions the Jerusalem council in Acts 15, and the fact that the Spirit came upon the Gentiles *as Gentiles* constitutes Peter's argument that the Gentiles need not be required to obey all the commandments of the Torah. While the Spirit's presence among both Jews and Gentiles powerfully illustrates and actualizes God's ever-expanding work in the world, it apparently does not erase the distinction—particularly with regard to stipulations of covenant faithfulness—between Jew and Gentile.

While the Spirit empowers Jews to uphold the "restraints, disciplines, and duties"[1] to which the Torah had always called them, the Spirit likewise orders the life of Gentile followers of Yeshua *so that* they may live as the people of God alongside and joined to the people of Israel. The practices that are required of Gentile believers in Acts 15 illustrate their turn from idolatry and arguably set basic parameters that enable table fellowship between Jews and Gentiles. Through God's work in their midst, Gentiles join into the teleological communal life of Israel without themselves becoming Jews.[2]

As you can see, this excerpt also addresses the issue of Jew/Gentile distinction, which I believe is indeed a central theme of the New Testament. In this regard, let us reflect for a moment on the central significance of the book of Acts within the New Testament canon. Consider the following explanation given by Mark Kinzer:

> David Trobisch argues that Acts of the Apostles performs an especially crucial function within the canon. According to Trobisch, the main concern of the final redaction of the New Testament is to minimize the conflict between Paul and the leaders of the Jerusalem *ekklēsia* (i.e., Peter, representing the Twelve, and James, representing the family of Jesus). Trobisch places Acts in this context: "Of all N.T. writings, it is the Book of Acts that most explicitly displays this harmonizing tendency." He goes so far as to suggest that the account of the Council of Jerusalem in Acts 15 "might even form the heart of the NT [New Testament]." Robert Wall agrees with Trobisch in his assessment of the canonical significance of Acts, though he emphasizes the *compatibility* of diverse

---

1. This is a reference to Donin's description of Shavuot. Donin, *To Be a Jew*, 240.

2. Rosner, "Witnesses."

apostolic viewpoints rather than their strict "harmonization": "The relations between James and Paul or between Peter and James as depicted at strategic moments in the plotline of Acts are generally collaborative rather than adversarial and frame the interpreter's approach to their biblical writings as essentially complementary (even though certainly not uniform and sometimes in conflict) in both meaning and function."

Moreover, the canonical placement of Acts before the letters of Paul implies that the framers of the canon intended the former to guide the interpretation of the latter. That is the reasonable conclusion reached by Brevard Childs:

[T]he canon has retained the Pauline letters, but within the framework of Acts which provides hermeneutical guidelines for their interpretation. The content of the letters of Paul and the portrayal of Acts are certainly not to be simply identified, nor can one be allowed to destroy the witness of the other. However, Acts instructs the community of faith in one direction in which to move by translating the significance of Paul's original life and message for a different generation of readers who did not share in Paul's historical ministry.

Scholars disagree about whether the author of Acts knew Paul personally and whether his portrait of the apostle to the gentiles is historically accurate. Regardless, the structure of the canon suggests that its framers wanted readers of the Pauline letters to take Acts into account when interpreting Paul's life, teaching, and purposes. Given the role Paul has played historically in shaping ecclesial attitudes towards Judaism, this hermeneutical function further emphasizes the importance of Acts for our concerns.[3]

As you can see, from my perspective, the ongoing significance of the Torah (and Israel's empowerment by the Spirit to obey Torah) thus has everything to do with Jew/Gentile distinction. Furthermore, as demonstrated in the excerpt above, I believe Paul must be read through the interpretive lens of Acts.

---

3. Kinzer, *Jerusalem Crucified*, 12–13.

On another note, you state that "I don't doubt that many of the first-generation Jewish believers did maintain a life of Torah. However, it is equally as clear that Torah observance was not maintained as the highest spiritual expression of their faith. That is why when the temple fell and Torah observance became impossible, that faith was able to thrive." What exactly do you mean by the phrase "highest spiritual expression of their faith"? Does this suggest that Torah observance was a matter of indifference for them? This reminds me of the Venn diagram question I raised before. What determines the extent to which a Spirit-led life is also a Torah-observant life, both for Yeshua's early followers and for us today? Also, with regard to your statement, the fact that the nascent Yeshua following movement was able to thrive post-70 AD seems unrelated to the role of Torah observance, as proto-rabbinic Judaism also took roots and eventually thrived without a Temple. I may be misunderstanding your point here, as I don't see the correlation you are making.

I'll leave it at that for now. As always, I look forward to hearing your response.

Jen

NOVEMBER 11, 2018

Jen,

Thank you for your important thoughts and questions. In regard to your point from Ezekiel that the Spirit will enable us to follow the "decrees" and "laws" of the Lord, I would, of course, agree. The point in Ezekiel, however, is not what form these decrees and laws will take in the new covenant era (keep in mind that some of the laws of Ezekiel's visionary temple depart from the Pentateuch); the point is only in regard to that which will help us in our obedience. I believe that it would have been impossible and unnecessary for God to reveal to Ezekiel what form of obedience or what manner of interaction with Torah this Spirit-indwelled people would have. For that understanding we must look to the New Testament Scriptures, that is, to those who actually experienced this outpouring and spoke or wrote with authority about it.

It seems to me that you and I are falling into the predictable patterns of those who debate the issues at hand. You are referring primarily to Acts and I to Paul (though, I believe, a close reading of Hebrews would also back up my perspective), and thus your defense of Acts as central brings up a highly relevant issue. I would argue for the primacy of Paul in laying a foundation for our understanding in these matters for the following reasons: 1) The argument for the placement of Acts after the Gospels as a lens on how to read Paul is a subjective conclusion since we do not know the motivations of the canonical framers. The placement of Acts may be according to the natural continuation of the gospel story. It would be odd to interrupt that narrative flow with several letters. Whatever the motive, as those who accept all of the books of the New Testament, our theology is formed by extracting from each book its full force and, where there are various understandings that could make sense, we limit our conclusions to those that align with other books. Thus, I would agree that Acts can serve as a lens on the Pauline corpus, but no more so than vice-versa; 2) Acts is a narrative that records the events and speeches of the nascent Messianic community. I do not disagree with the decision in Acts 15 for that particular situation, nor do I reject the idea that this decision is instructive for us today; however, before we decide how to apply it to modern circumstances, we must keep in mind the situation in which that decision was rendered and what other parts of the New Testament may have to say about the topic. While granting that Paul's letters were also situational, we must admit that the decisions of Acts 15 were highly influenced by circumstances that we do not share with that community. Those early Jewish believers considered continued Torah observance an obligation for themselves and not for the Gentiles. However, given that this group had the Temple, were surrounded by a community of those who were Torah-observant, given that they knew no other life or theology (using that term loosely) other than Temple-centered Torah observance, given that their sudden departure from a standardized Temple-centered Torah life would have sent a negative message in regard to Torah, and given their limited knowledge of the nascent Messianic faith (remember, they were just debating on whether believing Gentiles must convert or not), we cannot ascertain whether their manner of Torah observance was the eternal will of God for all believing Jewish people or simply the best possible decision for that particular group in that particular circumstance. Moreover, given the highly contextual nature of the council's letter to the Gentiles (given the opportunity to make a modern list of prohibitions for Gentile believers, would it parallel the list of verse 20?), it seems that the understanding of Messianic Jewish obedience in Acts 15 must also be understood contextually and not as an eternal dictate for first century-style Torah observance.

It seems to me that Acts' nature as a recording of events would need to be illuminated by other parts of our Scriptures (especially Paul) and by our own Spirit-led interaction with modern circumstances. Is, perhaps, the decision of Acts 15 an example that aligns with the thought of Hebrews 8:13, "In speaking of a new covenant, he makes the first one obsolete. And what is becoming obsolete and growing old is ready to vanish"? Even if we relegate this verse only to the Levitical sacrificial system, we must remember that it was this sacrificial system that (unlike today) was the heart of the Torah for our pre-70 ancestors. If we say that only the sacrificial system has changed and the rest remains intact, we are proposing an approach to Torah observance that the council in Acts 15 would not have understood, and that approach would be no less shocking to them than what I propose was Paul's direction. So, in understanding the applicability of the decision of Acts 15 for those of us in far-removed circumstances, I propose that we primarily look to the Gospels, Hebrews, and Paul to illuminate Acts rather than the other way around. Theirs could have been a decision based on an approach to Torah that was "becoming obsolete" and in our day without the Temple, such an approach may now be obsolete.

I was surprised by your statement that, "from my perspective, the ongoing significance of the Torah (and Israel's empowerment by the Spirit to obey Torah) . . . has everything to do with Jew/Gentile distinction." As I mentioned in my previous note, all things from my perspective find their value only in light of Messiah (John 3:16–21; Col 1:15–19). That Israel maintains an important and unique role in its witness to the Messiah is something about which we agree. However, the "one new man" of Ephesians 2 which is made possible through the "abolishing of commandments" (2:15) is also a testimony to the Messiah. The extent to which some are called to be a testimony through a life which emphasizes Jewish distinctiveness and others through a life that emphasizes the unity of Messiah's body is, I feel, not a matter of a theology that should dictate the dos and don'ts of the lives of individuals and far-flung communities. Rather, these callings should be a matter in which individuals, families, and local worship communities seek the guidance of the Spirit and Scripture for their particular situations. In addition, the method of maintaining a Jewish distinction, for those so called, can be through various means, as I mentioned in my previous letter.

Those who may feel the need to emphasize this distinction must remember that the distinction is not a clear commandment of our Messiah, nor is it mentioned as one of the fruits of the Spirit in

Galatians 5. This means that a focus on maintaining the distinction runs the risk of impinging upon things that are explicitly stated as goals, commandments, or marks of righteousness in the New Testament. One's focus on distinction must not, for example, violate the commandment to treat others the way one would want to be treated, nor should one emphasize distinction to the extent that the unity of the people of Messiah (the more important New Testament issue) is undermined.

Furthermore, if the testimony of distinction is a focus of one's spiritual expression, and if Torah observance is the manner in which that is to be maintained, it would seem that only a rabbinic method of Torah observance, as that which is observably Jewish to the modern world, would fit this category. Thus, sneaking onto the Temple Mount to sacrifice a Passover lamb would not fit this form of Torah observance, but praying the *Amidah* or doing good deeds in place of such a sacrifice would. Therefore, this rabbinic-style Messianic Jew must keep in mind that those things that are expressly Messianic (for example, that it is Yeshua and not prayer, good deeds, and repentance that replaces the sacrifices) are not innate to the rabbinic development of Torah minus Temple. In addition to not having cognizance of the implications on Torah observance in light of Messiah, the rabbinic approach to *halakha* is not overtly led by the Spirit (as the well-known Talmudic example of Aknai's oven demonstrates). Thus, the prophetic pronouncement of Ezekiel and others that the Spirit would heal our waywardness, a theme that Yeshua promises to fulfill in sending the Spirit, is being submitted to a form of Torah observance that replaces this theme of Spirit-indwelling with the authority of the legal decisions of the rabbis. It's not that the Spirit cannot covertly lead rabbinic decisions, although if the Spirit of God was the force behind Rabbinic Judaism, I assume that the Spirit would lead the rabbis to the Messiah (John 15:26). Nor would I claim that to follow rabbinic dictates is necessarily at odds with a Spirit-led life for everyone. But I would caution us against an encompassing pneumatology that would submit all believing Jews to an approach of Torah observance that is not, nor does it claim to be, the fulfillment of passages such as Ezekiel 36 and 37, especially given that the New

Testament makes it clear that a Spirit-led obedience is now available to us in Yeshua (John 7:39; Acts 2).

Thank you for your concluding questions and the opportunity to clarify my thoughts. You asked: "What exactly do you mean by the phrase 'highest spiritual expression of their faith'?" By "highest spiritual expression of faith" I mean that one can be strictly Torah-observant but not led by the Spirit and therefore not pleasing to God. One can refrain from adultery through the strength of the will, but to refrain out of love and a transformed mind in which one loves what God loves and hates what God hates is the work of the Spirit. The Torah does not go far enough. According to the Torah I can divorce my wife. Yeshua and the Spirit would lead me not to do so. According to the Torah I can expect compensation for damages. The rule of the Spirit would often have me be wronged rather than demand my rights (1 Cor 6:7). We are called to walk in the footsteps of the Messiah, especially in regard to the cross (Phil 2:5; 1 Pet 2:21). The cross was not the pinnacle of Messiah's Torah-observance but the pinnacle of his submission to the ongoing voice of God and the leading of the Spirit which descended on him at his immersion (Matt 3). In fact, as one who is hanged on a tree is cursed (Deut 21:21; Gal 3:13), it would seem that if Torah-observance were the pinnacle of Yeshua's life, he would have died some other way. Yet, for Yeshua (and so for us) the cross is the pinnacle of obedience to the Father, and this has nothing to do with Torah observance either in the literal reading of the Pentateuch or in its modern rabbinic expression. That Torah observance is not the pinnacle of our faith expression is also evident from the writings of Paul. "As for *Torah* righteousness" in his pre-Yeshua life, Paul was "blameless" (Phil 3:6). But this blameless life under Torah he now considers utterly sinful in the light of the new life he lives in the Spirit (1 Tim 1:13–15). In his former life, Paul was Torah-observant but still not pleasing to God.

You asked: "Does this suggest that Torah-observance was a matter of indifference for them?" I believe that the full working out of Yeshua's teaching and Paul's theology (and that of Hebrews) would lead not to the conclusion that Torah-observance was a matter of indifference, but that Torah observance (to the extent that it is equated with obedience to God) would be redefined and placed under the authority of Yeshua and the leading of the Spirit. Interaction with the literal text would be as important but more malleable than before, whereas guidance by the Spirit would take center stage and come with increased authority and clarity. The inner intent of Torah observance would not only be maintained but more gloriously revealed, while adherence to specific commandments would be subjected to this new and greater revelation. How this works out in a Venn diagram would, by the very nature of what I am proposing, depend on how the Spirit leads each individual, family, and local community. All would be Torah observant to a great extent (the Spirit will not lead us to commit murder or to worship an idol, etc.). None would be fully Torah observant (given the impossibility of obeying those commandments that require a temple), and none would be as Torah observant as they possibly can (if we could set up law courts that could adjudicate the stoning of Sabbath breakers and insist on levirate marriage, would this not now seem incongruent with the heart of New Testament teachings and with the reality of modern society?). One thing is sure, the Spirit would not lead us against God's righteous intentions that underlie the Torah (Rom 8:4). The New Testament defines that underlying intention of God in terms of love (Matt 7:12; 22:37–40; Rom 13:9–10). Nowhere in the New Testament is Torah summed up as a tool to keep Jews and Gentiles separated. If Torah observance is defined by God's intention and not necessarily the literal *mitzvot*, the Venn diagram would have two completely overlapping circles. If it is defined by a literal approach to the *mitzvot* or by a rabbinic approach to the *mitzvot*, how much the circles overlap will vary from individual to individual as the Spirit leads.

You said: "the fact that the nascent Yeshua following movement was able to thrive post-70 AD seems unrelated to the role of Torah observance, as proto-rabbinic Judaism also took roots and eventually thrived without a Temple." Proto-rabbinic Judaism thrived after the destruction of the Temple because it redefined Torah observance. I propose that the Yeshua movement thrived because literal Torah observance was not germane to its message. I also propose that it took an evil turn when most within it failed to understand that the pinnacle of their faith was to be led into Messiah-likeness by the Spirit. The body of Messiah must be defined as those who are transformed by the Spirit. Instead of a Spirit-indwelled people with a positive relationship to Torah, the Church largely became a people that replaced a Jewish law code with a Gentile/Christian law code.

Looking forward to your reply.
Josh

NOVEMBER 19, 2018

Josh,

With Regard to Your Point About Ezekiel

What you are proposing seems like some kind of free-for-all hermeneutic, where no particular concept or word is tethered to any concrete meaning. My understanding is that there is a consistent orbit of meaning throughout all of Scripture with regard to what Torah is. Yes, Paul's use of the word *nomos* is tricky in places, as it is clear that he is not always strictly referring to the covenantal Torah between Israel and God. That being said, teasing out the precise meaning of certain Pauline passages is quite different than denying that the term has a concrete meaning that endures throughout the text. While Paul may very well refer to different "laws" throughout his writing, I would strongly argue that in many cases he is in fact referring to Israel's Torah, as it has always been understood and was expressed in Paul's Second Temple context. This is an important point in our discussion because it unveils a fundamental difference between the way each of us approaches the text; you assume a sharp distinction between what Torah might mean in the context of the new covenant, while I assume that there is a large degree of continuity in its meaning throughout the text. (As a side note, you made a similar comment about the impossibility of defining the term Pharisee in the first century. Once again, while there are valuable and legitimate debates about fine points of definition, to simply claim the term is vacuous and meaningless sidesteps any kind of fruitful dialogue, not to mention dismisses many volumes of relevant and credible scholarship).

NOVEMBER 19, 2018

With Regard to Your Points Concerning Paul and Acts

First, I have seen the book of Acts all too readily dismissed as unhistorical (and thus somehow irrelevant?) by renowned New Testament scholars. My belief in the inspiration of the biblical text (which I imagine you share) does not allow me to draw such a flat conclusion. From my perspective, one of the great strengths of the new/radical new perspective on Paul is that it finally provides a viable solution for harmonizing Paul's letters and Acts. This does not necessarily mean there are no "mistakes" in Acts, and that the corrective function of Paul and Acts doesn't go both ways. However, I am quite convinced that the canonical order of the New Testament texts is significant and intentional, as I stated in my last letter. Along these lines, I also read Acts not only as a record of historical events, but as a carefully crafted document whose goal is to communicate a particular theological message.[1]

Second, it seems to me that you're treating Acts 15 too flippantly. The primacy of the Jerusalem community is well established[2] and clearly acknowledged even by Paul himself. Therefore, a decision such as the one in this chapter ought to hold a great deal of authority. Furthermore, if you're arguing that it was decreed for a specific group under a specific set of circumstances, doesn't this set of conditions also apply to just about all of Paul's statements? Why wouldn't we also dismiss them as purely contextual and not universally valid or binding?

In any case, if you have a particular concern with giving Paul hermeneutical priority, and with New Testament rulings being context-specific, let's introduce another key text for discussion: Paul's "rule in all the churches" (1 Cor. 7:17ff). This seems to be about as universal as an epistle proclamation can be. It is clear that circumcision is shorthand for Torah observance for Paul (Rom 2:25), so this passage once again seems to a) uphold Torah observance for Jewish Yeshua believers, and b) reinforce an ongoing Jew/Gentile distinction.

---

1. See Kinzer, *Jerusalem Crucified*, 10–15.

2. For an excellent treatment of this topic, see Richard Bauckham's essay "James and the Jerusalem Community" in Skarsaune and Hvalvik, *Jewish Believers*.

With Regard to Your Proposed Reading of Ephesians 2

Given what you've said, it seems like your understanding of Paul's phrase "one new man" is actually "one new Gentile." What, if anything, endures of the Jewish nature and character of the *ekklesia* you are describing? From my perspective, one of the most remarkable aspects of Messiah's work is a visible reconciliation between Jew and Gentile, which we see manifesting itself in the *ekklesia*. The entire narrative of the Tanakh is punctuated by conflict and strife between Israel and the nations, and it is only through Messiah that this perpetual hostility is finally reconciled. However, this glorious accomplishment can only serve as a sign to the world if Jews and Gentiles in the *ekklesia* are visibly identifiable as such.

Furthermore, according to the antinomian hermeneutic you are proposing, how could Torah observance possibly be a matter of personal choice or pneumatological leading? If indeed life in the Spirit is sharply juxtaposed to Torah, and Paul reiterates repeatedly that the era of Torah has now passed, wouldn't it then be *contrary* to life in the new covenant to go back to that antiquated, flawed, incarcerating law? As you know, this argument is well trod in patristic theology, and the church fathers quite logically declare that any continued observance of Torah is "like a dog returning to its vomit." For example, in the words of Ignatius: "Put aside then the evil leaven, which has grown old and sour, and turn to the new leaven, which is Jesus Christ . . . It is monstrous to talk of Jesus Christ and to practice Judaism."[3] If Paul's view of the law is as you state, shouldn't Ignatius' statement then be the natural conclusion?

With Regard to Your Comments on Rabbinic Tradition

It is, of course, obvious that the rabbis throughout the ages who have served as the architects of rabbinic tradition have not been Yeshua followers. However, I view rabbinic tradition in much the same light as church tradition; both movements have been led by God, and both movements are deeply flawed. One of the great challenges

---

3. Ignatius, *Mag.*, 10:2–3.

of the Messianic Jewish movement is that we must carefully discern how, where and when to submit ourselves to each, and how, when and where we must take a stand against each. We certainly should not uncritically adopt all rabbinic practices. And neither should we give church tradition such blanket authority. It is indeed the discernment of the Spirit (and the model of Messiah) that ought to guide us through this conundrum, and to make known to us where each tradition has gone astray.

On this note, many modern evangelicals are often quick to disavow any allegiance to or influence by church tradition, but I believe this move is naïve and ultimately dishonest. Evangelical theology is clearly marked by the imprint of orthodox Christology (as determined by the church councils), and the tenor of evangelical identity is deeply determined by the Protestant ethos. So, whether we like it or not, we are a product of history. As Messianic Jews, I would argue that we are a product of *both* church tradition and rabbinic tradition, and it is our unique responsibility and legacy to both embody and critique both. They are like our two feuding parents, and we are left to forge our own identity with their blood running in our veins.

As a final and related note, I take exception to your statement that "one can be strictly Torah observant but not led by the Spirit and therefore not pleasing to God." Does this automatically imply that all of the faithful, devout Jews in the world who don't follow Yeshua are displeasing to God? Do their good deeds of charity and faithfulness amount to nothing in God's economy? I find your claim to be particularly problematic in light of the deeply troubled history between Christianity and Judaism, and the gentilized, supersessionist Jesus that has been proclaimed to the Jewish people throughout the centuries, often accompanied by a life or death ultimatum.

I look forward to your reply.
Jen

NOVEMBER 23, 2018

Shalom Jen,

Thanks again for your thoughts.

In regard to your comments on my approach to Ezekiel, I would argue for the transmutability of exact Torah commandments, and I would say that so did Ezekiel (the practices in his visionary temple do not always match those in the Torah), so do the rabbis, and so do all with a reasonable approach to Torah. No one except the most extreme argues for a literal return to all of the Torah *mitzvot*. No one except the most extreme stone rebellious children and homosexuals, throw out mixed fabric clothing, etc. The extent to which Torah has changed under the rabbis is rather acute in many areas. In rabbinic interpretation, lighting Shabbat candles is Torah but believing in the continuing need for blood atonement (something that the gospel rests upon) is not. I don't say this in judgment of Judaism but in defense of my understanding of Ezekiel. I would also say that what comes across in your writing is not so much a desire for the "laws" and "rulings" of Ezekiel to mean the same thing that they meant to Moses, but to find a modern approach to Judaism that is recognizably Jewish without holding up each rabbinic decision against an unchanging understanding of "laws" and "rulings." What I am saying is not a "free-for-all hermeneutic" but rather a firm faith that Yeshua and the writers of the New Testament understood and emphasized the heart of the Torah and that they did a better job at revealing Torah than anyone else. If the individual laws of Torah are pliable under the rabbis, then they can also be so under the guidance of the Spirit. Once we understand the extent to which we cannot follow the Torah literally, the more we'll understand that the issue is not how Torah observant to be, but whose voice to listen to for modern application. The intent of the "laws" and "rulings" are fully upheld in my understanding of the New Testament, even if the application of such looks different than Ezekiel could have imagined.

Similarly, my point about Acts and Paul's claim to be a Pharisee was not that this term had no meaning, but that the term as it was used in Acts 23 should be confined to the emphasis with which Paul used it. If I used your hermeneutic it seems as if I could say that Paul was a Pharisee and therefore did not believe in Yeshua because the Pharisaic line was to reject him as the Messiah. That, of course, is not what Paul meant by that term in that context. I was simply saying that it was an over-application to use that passage to show that Paul's theology toward Torah was the same as that of the Pharisees. Even if his observant life was much the same (and this is debated), his theology was not. His language about Torah in some places has no parallel in any rabbinic writings or Pharisaic traditions. Since the exact border lines between "Pharisee" and "not a Pharisee" are largely not known to us, we should restrict ourselves in how we see Paul applying that term to himself by the given situation.

With regard to your comments on Acts 15, I did not mean to dismiss Acts as a theological book. However, because it is a narrative, it is very easy to read our already formed theologies into it. Eisegesis is always a concern, and particularly so when looking for theology in narratives. Therefore, one must only carefully step outside of the main point of the pericope. There is no doubt that the main thrust of Acts 15 is not that Messianic Jews should remain observant, but that Gentiles should not be pressured to do so. Messianic Jewish observance is an assumption, but there is a theme in Acts that a spirituality based on faith in Yeshua is overshadowing the traditional concerns of Torah observance, even for Jews. "Why then do you put God to the test by putting a yoke on the neck of the disciples (i.e., Torah observance)—which neither our fathers nor we have been able to bear? But instead, we believe that we are saved through the grace of the Lord Yeshua, in the same way as they are" (Acts 15:10–11). Is this a hint that the heavy yoke of traditional halakhic concerns will eventually be thrown off, even for Jewish believers? At the least, it shows that the grace of Yeshua is a more important topic than Torah. Also consider Acts 13:38–39:

"Therefore, let it be known to you, brothers, that through this One is proclaimed to you the removal of sins, including all those from which you could not be set right by the *Torah* of Moses. Through this One everyone who keeps trusting is made righteous." And we see this theme by the fact that the driving force of the Acts narrative is solely the gospel. For example, Paul's final journey to Jerusalem is not for the sake of visiting the Temple, but in order to deliver the gospel to his countrymen (Acts 21:13). Torah observance for Messianic Jews may be assumed by the council in Acts 15, but the driving force of the book is the gospel (as it should be for us). I think it's right to assume that Torah observance must yield to this new and more powerful revelation.

I agree with your point about Paul's letters also being context-driven, but in terms of an evolving theology of Torah, Paul has an advantage for us over Acts 15 in the following way. If we are to assume that the understanding of the Jerusalem council of Acts was that Jews should maintain Torah, and that for them Torah observance meant what it meant for most other Jews (especially in regard to seeing the Temple as central), then we must conclude that according to their understanding the Temple is important for our spiritual/theological/Jewish expression. That is, we would be limited in our spiritual expression if we lacked a Temple, for that was the crown and center of our Torah observance. However, as I read Paul and Hebrews, I get no sense at all that our spiritual expression should be considered limited without a Temple. One question that I think you should consider is why neither Paul nor the book of Hebrews alludes to the importance of the Temple for our spirituality (and this aligns with John 4:21–24). To reemphasize: nothing in Paul's and Hebrews' spirituality is limited by the lack of a Temple nor is the Temple even mentioned in passages that encourage us to reach for our spiritual potential. If Paul's writings are situational (and they are), there is still a ready applicability of his theology for us that the common understanding of Acts 15 lacks; that is, we can fully embrace Paul (and Hebrews) without having to re-decipher his words into our Temple-less context.

I want to thank you for your point regarding Ephesians 2 because it has made me aware that I have either not been communicating my position well or I have not been repeating my pro-Torah points enough so as to keep me out of the camp of those who actually are antinomian in their theology. To call my view antinomian is to miss both my parallels with the pliability of Torah under any Temple-less system (including Rabbinic Judaism) and the mirror image of your own view. That is, if I am antinomian because I would submit Torah observance to being led by the Spirit, then we would also have to conclude that you are against following the Spirit because you would have our guidance by the Spirit submitted to a form of literal Torah observance. As it is, I don't consider myself antinomian and I don't consider you to be against following the Spirit. The question is not whether to throw out the Torah or the Spirit, but rather which of these takes precedence and guides the other in the new covenant era. For me, it seems clear from the New Testament that Torah is subjected to and malleable before the Spirit.

I am pro-Torah in that it remains fully intact as a revelation of the wisdom of God. I have never taught that to follow many of its rules, be they ceremonial, cultural, or ethical, is wrong. I think my previous letters will show that. However, when Torah is presented as a written, in force law code, that *approach* is antithetical in Paul's theology to being led by the Spirit. It is this understanding that makes Paul's letters and Paul's activities in Acts reconcilable. Torah is not a negative, but an approach to Torah that will not allow its rules and laws to bend to the leading authority of the Spirit is unacceptable in light of our New Testament existence (for a case of this proper approach in the Tanakh, see Hezekiah's Passover in 2 Chronicles 30). When Paul contrasts Torah observance with being led by the Spirit, the contrast is between Torah observance by the letter without the Spirit versus obedience to God that is informed by Scripture but led by the Spirit.

I am pro-Torah in its ultimate aims, especially that of love. I am pro-Torah in that many of its specific laws can remain applicable and that the Spirit can lead people (myself included) to follow different rulings. However, a legal approach to Torah is by definition different than being led by the Spirit. If your ox gores my donkey, rather than automatically running out to collect the damages accorded me by the Torah, I will seek the leading of the Spirit. Perhaps this is an opportunity to show a Messiah-like love and relieve you of any debt. The higher expression of my faith is the latter and not the former. My main spiritual hope is that the Spirit will make me more like Yeshua in regard to his ethics and love. To the extent that Torah helps that, it is a blessing. To the extent that it tries to take primacy over this form of spirituality, it is a hindrance. The pinnacle of our history and the pinnacle of God's self-revelation is no longer Sinai, but the ministry of Yeshua and the outpouring of the Spirit; our spiritual lives should reflect this.

To answer your questions: "What, if anything, endures of the Jewish nature and character of the *ekklesia* you are describing?" Much endures. The coming of the Messiah was a Jewish event. The giving of the Spirit was and is a Jewish event prophesied for Israel by the Jewish prophets in which both Jew and Gentile can now participate. The Scriptures of this *ekklesia* are also Jewish. The very nature of the *ekklesia* by its worship of Yeshua, the indwelling of the Spirit, and its guiding Scriptures is Jewish whether or not these things are recognized as distinctly Jewish in our day. The accusation that I'm describing "one new Gentile" is because you are using modern, Western definitions of Jew and Gentile. No one in the time of the New Testament would see the attributes I mentioned above as characteristically Gentile in nature. Within those broad but definitely Jewish descriptions of the *ekklesia* there is freedom and, at many times encouragement, for more precise Jewish expressions such as keeping kosher, honoring the seventh day Sabbath, celebrating the festivals, and adhering to some rabbinic norms such as lighting the Shabbat candles. As long as these things point to the broader realities of the *ekklesia*, they can be quite beneficial.

My reluctance to espouse a theology in which Messianic Jews must participate in a more noticeably Jewish expression and non-Jewish Christians must not is precisely because of the pedestal on which I place being led by the Spirit. Can I say that in every instance a Jewish believer must and a non-Jewish believer must not follow expressly Jewish religious and cultural norms? I am in no way prepared to make that blanket statement, so even if it may be generally true, and even if it may be the way in which the Spirit often leads Jews and non-Jews, I still prefer to leave Torah observance under the umbrella of Spirit-guidance rather than theology, especially when I feel that an over-preoccupation with being Jewish or non-Jewish is a distraction from the true focus of the New Testament which is to live a transformed life of love in the Spirit that glorifies our Messiah.

While I don't believe that the main thrust of the Tanakh is Jewish and Gentile hostility (much more space is allotted to Israel's tenuous relationship with God), I still see a distinction between Jew and Gentile as something from which an important message of Messiah's reconciliation can be revealed. However, the main point of 1 Corinthians 7:17–21 is not the importance of distinction (otherwise, Paul say would not have said that "circumcision is nothing and uncircumcision is nothing,") but making sure that no one thinks that something is spiritually gained by converting to or from Judaism. That is, Paul's main concern was that the gospel message remains sufficient without having to add to it an identity marker such as "Jew" or "Gentile." However, within that larger context he does ask the Jew to remain a Jew and the Gentile a Gentile. I would only add that in the age of the Spirit we allow God to guide each one in how to do that. We must not sacrifice demonstrating Messiah's inclusive and loving character as the Shepherd who makes "one flock" from Israel and the nations (John 10:16) for the false impression that his plan of demonstrating reconciliation within the *ekklesia* is only possible if we submit the Jewish side to a method of Torah observance that conflicts with the primacy of being led by the Spirit. Neither should we ask the Gentile side to actively avoid Jewish expressions to which the Spirit may be calling.

Just to tie up a few loose ends . . . I agree with your penultimate paragraph on Messianic Judaism being the recipient of two competing parents. We are in a unique situation to be able to receive from and critique both traditions. However, we must not see the institutional church and Rabbinic Judaism as our only progenitors. There is also a history of renewal movements within Jewish and Christian contexts that we must examine.

Your understanding that my view should logically lead to something parallel to Ignatius' anti-Jewish view was answered earlier in this letter, but to clarify: I can only be perceived as being anti-Torah if by that we mean a legal approach versus a spiritual approach to the Pentateuch. In other words, I am against a Spirit-less black and white approach to Torah that runs out to put a border around my roof in fulfillment of Deuteronomy 22:8 instead of an approach in which Yeshua's teachings and the guidance of the Spirit teaches me how to apply that verse so that I make my entire home safe for family and visitors. Additionally, I am against an approach to life that emphasizes obedience to law above heart transformation by the Spirit.

In response to your last paragraph in which you took exception to my statement that "one can be strictly Torah observant but not led by the Spirit and therefore not pleasing to God," let me respond with a question. Do you think that if I put a border around my roof but fail to allow the Spirit to lead me to fix my broken stairs or my faulty electrical wiring, that I'm being pleasing to God? I imagine that your answer would be no, and that you would say that a strict understanding of Torah observance in that case is not good enough. I imagine that almost all rabbis would also agree. I did not categorize all Judaism and all our ancestors as unrighteous or unspiritual. They, like we, stand before God who weighs the intentions of the heart, something that I am unprepared to do in either a positive or negative fashion. I will say that the book of John contrasts those who do wicked things with those who do works of truth that are "carried out in God" (John 3:20–21), and that those who do these true works in God will come to the light (which, in the book of John, is Yeshua). It seems to me that there would be many of our people who would not blindly do the right thing but do true works *in God* and that the evidence for these works would be seen in the way they respond to the light. However, to assume that literal Torah observance is enough is not only a step outside of the gospel message, it is also not in alignment with the prophets and rabbis who criticize rote obedience that lacks heart.

At the same time, I do not feel that Paul was shadow boxing. His emphasis on the Spirit in contrast to a legalistic approach to righteousness shows two things. First, it shows that there must have been a strong contingent of those who sought righteousness through a legalistic approach to Torah. Second, it shows that the outpouring of the Spirit came in such power that any possibility of following

Torah as a legal document rather than the leading of the Spirit should have been demolished. One can scarcely read 2 Corinthians 3, or any number of New Testament passages, without coming to the conclusion that a glorious, more spiritual day is upon us. We cannot minimize the glory of Messiah or the radical life in the Spirit to which we are called in order to curtail our differences with Rabbinic Judaism or in order to glorify our status as the circumcised. The answer is not to condemn Judaism, nor is it to eschew many of the beautiful things within it, but neither is the answer to water down the profound nature of our faith to atone for the evil vehemence of too many errant "Christian" teachers of the past. We must speak the truth in love and humility, even if the radical nature of our faith will cause us to be rejected. If we think that our message is not profoundly different than any other system (including Rabbinic Judaism) then the conflicts presented in the gospels and epistles get watered down to meaningless misunderstandings. Yeshua's and the disciples' clashes with the Jewish religious leaders were not primarily about a failure of the leaders to understand the gospel; there are substantive differences that must not be glossed over.

There are certain figures in our history that radically altered the religious life of our ancestors, of which Moses and David would be the prime examples. One does not follow Abraham as if the ministry of Moses had not taken place. One should not follow Moses as if God did not make a new covenant with David. For those who follow him, the ministry of Yeshua leaves an even more indelible mark on the way we interact with all that came before. It is grossly limiting to say that Yeshua's only role was that of instructor and atoner. The emphasis of much of the New Testament is that these roles led to the outpouring of the Spirit. If we approach Torah as if this latter event did not produce dramatic change, then we may be in danger of minimizing our participation in it and limiting our own blessing and the blessing of others who need our supernatural testimony.

I look forward to your reply.

Shalom,
Josh

NOVEMBER 28, 2018

Josh,

Thank you for your thoughtful and articulate clarification of your position. Much of what you wrote resonates with me.

It seems to me that one of the big issues yet to be teased out that lies behind much of our conversation is the role of rabbinic tradition. Several times you have emphasized the issue of "modern application" of Torah and who we look to as interpretive authorities in this regard. Yes, we have the New Testament text and the interpretive precedent of Paul, the Jerusalem Council, etc. However, as you state, our situation is much different than theirs, not least because of the absence of the Temple.

Because Christianity quickly became overtly and unrelentingly anti-Jewish, the Christian tradition has left us no living model of how to follow Yeshua and live faithfully as Jews. Quite the opposite; Christian tradition has all too often echoed Ignatius, insisting that any ongoing adherence to Jewish custom or practice is antithetical to following Yeshua.

I believe that God's covenant with Israel is irrevocable, and that the *ketuba* between God and Israel is Torah. I see it as our unique heritage and legacy to live out the distinctive calling of our people and be a witness to God in the world by doing so. Our embracing this covenant is all the more powerful because of our recognition of and love for Messiah.

But in living out this calling as the people of Israel, we are indelibly bound to the rabbis. While the Spirit may absolutely lead us to challenge and even reject certain rabbinic rulings, I believe we are deeply indebted to the chain of rabbis who have faithfully preserved the Jewish tradition that the church has repeatedly attempted to destroy and stomp out. If we want to discern what it looks like to live as Messianic Jews today, I posit that we cannot do so in a way that disregards the rabbis and the living heritage they have guarded and perpetuated over the centuries.

I don't believe we as a community have the authority to single-handedly define or embody what Judaism truly is. We are called to show the world what it looks like to live as Jewish followers of Messiah in our day and age, but we are not at liberty to create an entirely new definition of Judaism and expect it to have any kind of authority or legitimacy.

Just as church tradition has bequeathed to us the boundaries of orthodox theology, Jewish tradition has bequeathed to us the parameters of Jewish orthopraxy. Because each tradition did so in a spirit of intentional hostility toward the other, we have much to critique about each. But we are also equally bound to each. Just as we cannot dismiss the Spirit-led affirmations of the Nicene Creed (even while we decry the vehement anti-Judaism of Constantine and the glaring omissions within the Creed itself), so too we cannot dismiss the longsuffering dedication of the rabbis to preserve a distinct and faithful halakhic tradition.

In my opinion, what it means to be Messianic Jews is to live in the tension of these two great yet flawed religious traditions, each of which believes with an air of supremacy that it has no need of the other. What it means to be Messianic Jews is to stand in the chasm left by the "parting of the ways" and declare that we refuse to choose between Christianity without Judaism or Judaism without Messiah. Our role is to prophetically protest against the either/or framework that history has offered to us and be a visible sign that there is indeed another way, and that it is the way of our Jewish Messiah and the early architects of his community.

In doing so, we are absolutely declaring that Torah observance minus Messiah is inadequate. But so too are we declaring that discipleship to Messiah minus Israel's covenantal particulars is deficient. Yes, the meaning of Torah is not fixed and unchanging, and every new context demands a new layer of modern application. But as Messianic Jews, we have no precedence or authority for implementing this process without the rabbis.

In saying this, I am arguing that God has been guiding the chain of rabbinic tradition in the same way he has been guiding the church. Both communities are his covenant people, and both are sinning against him by their rejection of and hostility toward the other. Nonetheless, he is faithful to and present amidst both. Along these lines, I wholeheartedly concur with Mark Kinzer's statement that, "in light of the church's history of supersessionism, anti-Judaism, and violent persecution . . . the Jewish no to Yeshua becomes a sign of his presence in Israel rather than of his absence."[1]

The high calling of our movement is to begin to bring healing to this tragic history and to demonstrate another way, one that puts Messiah at the center of Torah and reminds the world that Yeshua is indeed our greatest rabbi.

So, yes, I am attempting to "find a modern approach to Judaism that is recognizably Jewish." Are you seeking the same thing? How does your vision for our community differ from what I've expressed here?

Jen

---

1. Kinzer, *Postmissionary*, 225–226.

DECEMBER 3, 2018

Jen,

As always, great thoughts and questions. I believe that the heart of the issue around which we have been dancing is our take on Rabbinic Judaism, so I am glad that you have identified that. It may seem that if it is as you have said, that God has been guiding the church in matters of orthodoxy and the rabbinic sages in matters of orthopraxy, then Messianic Judaism is (or should be) a beautiful marrying of the two together. However, I think the issue is more complicated.

The question is not whether Rabbinic Judaism is as you say. Given my firm belief in God's continuing love for Israel and his manner of working in human affairs regardless of if or how he is acknowledged, I do not doubt that God has been leading the rabbis to some extent. However, can we conclude that, even if there is some guidance of the Spirit among those who deny Yeshua, God necessarily leads those who acknowledge Yeshua in the same way? In other words, the point that God has been leading non-Messianic Israel does not necessarily lead to the conclusion that we Messianics must do as non-Messianic Israel does.

I am not proposing a wholesale eschewal of Rabbinic Judaism. Nor, as I've stated, am I ruling out the possibility that individual Messianic Jews or even Messianic Jewish communities can be led by the Spirit to follow rabbinic *halakha* to various degrees. However, this must be under the umbrella of being led by the Spirit and not a blanket religious mandate even if, as is often claimed, knowledge of Yeshua and the indwelling of the Spirit "enlivens" traditional observance. I think this for two reasons. First, rabbinic ordinances are so all-encompassing (how one eats, prays, dresses, studies, etc.) that the question one would constantly have to ask oneself is not "how is the Spirit leading me," but "am I in compliance with the *halakha*?" And when one is unsure of the manner of conduct that they should be exhibiting, to whom or what do they turn for wisdom? Must we pour through pages of Talmudic commentaries and rabbinic responsa to make an informed decision, or should we turn to God in prayer and Spirit-led Bible study? For human guidance in spiritual matters, should I consult those with a vast repository of rabbinic wisdom or the humble person who regularly hears from God? I'm not assuming that someone can't fit both of those categories; the point is to question which attribute is the more important. So my first concern is about the practicality of following an exhaustive system of rules while simultaneously being led by the Spirit in matters of daily living.

My second and similar concern is this: do the spiritual goals of the rabbinic system overlap with the goals of the New Testament? On a broad level, we could say yes. Both approaches seek to be pleasing to God, to extol him in worship, and to live in light of his mercy and faithfulness. However, there are matters of the new covenant that are alien to Rabbinic Judaism, and often those matters that are the most unique to new covenant faith are also of the utmost importance. In particular, the New Testament emphasizes the importance of the unity of Jew and Gentile in Messiah. Rabbinic Judaism makes a point of keeping a spiritual barrier between Jews and Gentiles. The unfettered proclamation of Yeshua is another unique goal of the new covenant. These are not peripheral issues, nor are they simply matters of theology; these are fundamental differences that will have an impact on *halakha*.

I suppose I'm seeing something in your letters that strikes me as inconsistent. It may not be, but it strikes me as such, and I respectfully ask if you could clarify. In claiming that we can largely follow the church in matters of orthodoxy and largely follow Rabbinic Judaism in matters of orthopraxy, you seem to be promoting a non-holistic understanding to our religious expression. That is, you seem to propose that our *halakha* is not so intimately tied to our theology that we can't have vastly different theologies with another group while simultaneously having vastly similar manners of living, and not just similar manners of living in a broad sense (don't kill, be faithful to your spouse, etc.), but the adoption of a very specific and controlled manner of living and worship. It would seem to me, therefore, that you are arguing that one's theology lives a separate life from one's *halakha*. And yet it is the tool of theology that you are using to contend for making orthodox *halakha* more normative for Messianic Jewish expression. You are not contending for orthodox expression based on cultural concerns or physical health, for example, but because you think that theology demands it. But if theology demands a way of living in this case, why does theology not naturally demand a way of living in all aspects to the extent that a different *halakha* will naturally be born out of a different theology?

The above may seem like semantics, but here lies the heart of it for me. I want to be so in love with the theological revelation given to me in the new covenant that every other part of my life flows from it. Is Yeshua God revealed in the flesh? Is the Holy Spirit poured out because of his sacrifice? Is he the new High Priest with a new covenant? Is he the newly revealed authority over Torah? Can we adhere to a theology that answers these questions affirmatively and expect that we live Jewish lives in the classical sense when the guiding voices for the classical sense would answer all of those questions in the negative? These are not differences akin to the disputes of the schools of Shammai and Hillel; these are towering truths that demand certain life responses that don't fit into systems that deny them. I would point out the life of Yeshua. I believe that if we picture him largely fitting in with the Pharisees (the sect he probably most overlapped with) we are missing the point of the gospels when they remind us through conflict passages that his essence was too great to fit into any system and that all must either bow to him or be in conflict with him (Matt 21:44).

Now, I could ask a completely different but also important set of questions. Does not our theology affirm that God is faithful to Israel? Does not our theology affirm that God loves Israel and has a continuing plan for her? It is because I would answer yes to these questions that supersessionism and the history of the church's anti-Judaism are egregious to me. If our *halakha* is to be intimately tied to our theology, it should also reflect these pro-Israel truths. To rein in the move of the Spirit so that I will only follow if it rejects all things Jewish is more dangerous than insisting that the Spirit can only lead me along the lines of Orthodox Judaism. However, I don't believe that either extreme is warranted. One extreme denies the Spirit's guidance in terms of God's continuing love for Israel, the other extreme, I would argue, denies the Spirit's guidance in terms of a *halakha* that rightly honors our new High Priest. "For whenever the priesthood is altered, out of necessity an alteration of law also takes place" (Heb 7:12). We must allow the Spirit to guide us in terms of this newness, but we must also allow the Spirit to lead us in honoring God's ancient and enduring love for Israel.

You asked the following: "I am attempting to 'find a modern approach to Judaism that is recognizably Jewish.' Are you seeking the same thing? How does your vision for our community differ from what I've expressed here?"

I'm afraid my goal is simpler. When I was younger, I very much wanted to do what you are attempting in finding the right (often called "balanced" or "mature") approach for Messianic Judaism. I especially focused on the area of prayer. I spent many hours poring over traditional *siddurim*, reading books on liturgy, and reworking (several times over) a Messianic *siddur* that I had hoped would help define our movement in terms of liturgical worship. I am not seeking that anymore. My hope in terms of my personal ministry is only that through my teaching, example, and prayers people will gain a greater vision of who Yeshua is and what his work has done so that they worship in spirit and in truth (John 4:23), bear the fruit of the Spirit (Gal 5:22–23), demonstrate the unity of all believers (John 17:21), and share in the Spirit's love for Israel. How kosher each kitchen should be or how liturgical each Messianic congregation should be is something I would prefer to leave to the guidance of the Spirit.

My greatest fear for our movement is not that we won't be Jewish enough, but that we won't follow the Spirit in all matters, that we'll be led by pro- or anti-Orthodox sentiments rather than God's voice, that in the clutter of arguments over Torah observance we'll forget that the Spirit really can lead us if we take the time to listen with submitted hearts and open Bibles. My measure of success for a Messianic synagogue is no longer in judging how well it integrates Jewish *halakha* with Messianic truths, but how alive it is in the Spirit and how effortlessly its worship expressions flow from its fecund theology. My vision is by its very nature less precise than one that follows the well-trodden path of rabbinic dictates. Whether this following of the Spirit leads to something that adheres enough to classical Judaism to rightly be called Judaism is less important to me than whether we are living in the full force of our theological convictions with regard to the Messianic and spiritual truths that include new realities but an old and enduring love for the people of Israel.

If God needs the world to see a distinctly and unequivocally Jewish people acknowledging Yeshua, he can do that with a revival among secular Israelis who need not adopt an iota of orthodox *halakha* to show their Jewishness. My point is only that our call is simply to be obedient to the Spirit, not to try to figure out and rescue God's plan. If we take too much upon ourselves and find out that we were mistaken, the consequences can be disastrous. So, let us err on the side of love, humility, inclusiveness, and obedience to the Spirit. It is difficult for me to imagine God, to the extent I understand his nature, being upset with us for maintaining these attributes above all else.

One last note. You state the following: "The high calling of our movement is to begin to bring healing to this tragic history and to demonstrate another way, one that puts Messiah at the center of Torah and reminds the world that Yeshua is indeed our greatest rabbi." I agree completely with the first part of this statement, and I think that our freedom in following the Spirit as it enlivens our lives and the biblical texts will draw Jews and Christians into a love for one another. While I don't disagree with the latter part of this statement, I might place the emphasis elsewhere. Yeshua is indeed "at the center of Torah" and he is indeed "our greatest rabbi." More importantly, Torah is found in Messiah and "He is the image of the invisible God" (Co 1:15). This emphasis places Yeshua over Judaism rather than within it. I know from previous conversations that your Christology is quite high, but I wonder if, perhaps subconsciously, your desire to place Yeshua-faith within contemporary Judaism has caused you to prefer muted expressions (Yeshua within Torah,

Yeshua as rabbi) that can be seen as more compatible with it, rather than more potent expressions which Rabbinic Judaism would reject not only because they are placed on Yeshua, but because they renounce the very concept of a fully divine messianic figure. But perhaps I'm reading too much into your word choices in this one sentence.

As always, I look forward to your response.

Respectfully,
Josh

JANUARY 6, 2018

Josh,

As always, thank you for your thoughtful and articulate letter. While much of our conversation so far has focused most sharply on biblical and related theological issues, we now seem to be teasing out the ecclesiological and missiological implications of those concepts. Let me thus reply to the vision you have presented, which will in turn further highlight the difference between our respective stances.

You ask, "can we conclude that, even if there is some guidance of the Spirit among those who deny Yeshua, he necessarily leads those who acknowledge Yeshua in the same way? In other words, the point that God has been leading non-Messianic Israel does not necessarily lead to the conclusion that we Messianics must do as non-Messianic Israel does." Because I see the people of Israel—of which Messianic Jews are a part—as commanded by God to live in a particular, distinctive way in the world, I believe that the Spirit's leading of Rabbinic Judaism absolutely also applies to Messianic Jews. I don't believe that our application of rabbinic tradition will look exactly the same as any of the other branches of Judaism, because our observance must always be carried out in light of Messiah's self-revelation. But the fact that Messiah constitutes our hermeneutical lens on rabbinic tradition does not unhitch us from its authority and power. It simply means that our commitment to Yeshua informs our wrestling with how to live as Jews. The reality is that, because church tradition has developed in overt hostility toward Jewish practice and identity, we ought to stand in gratitude to God for safeguarding, preserving and guiding halakhic standards by means of the rabbis.

Because this is my view, I don't perceive the questions "how is the Spirit leading me?" and "am I in compliance with the *halakha*?" to be starkly distinct, as you do. Because the Spirit is indeed the Spirit of Israel's God, released into the world through the work of Israel's Messiah, I don't believe the Spirit leads us away from Judaism, but deeper into its heart and meaning. So while there may be points of sharp distinction between our observance and that of non-Yeshua believing Jews, I believe the area of overlap should be much greater than you seem to allow for. I don't believe it is the exceptional case that individual Messianic Jews would be led to live halakhic lives; rather, I believe that in exceptional cases the Spirit leads us to step away from or disregard *halakha*. I say this because I believe we still constitute part of *am yisrael* (the people of Israel), and thereby are called to live according to the specific ordinances commissioned to our people.

With regard to your concern about the New Testament emphasis on "the importance of the unity of Jew and Gentile in Messiah," I fully uphold the central significance of said unity, but I do not think it in any way eliminates the *distinction* between Jew and Gentile and the correlative callings that accompany those identities. So, yes to unity, no to uniformity. In fact, the marked difference between Jew and Gentile is precisely what makes unity so meaningful and powerful. After all, isn't a harmonious marriage remarkable on account of the vast differences between men and women? In both cases, it is the presence of significant difference that makes unity so mighty.

As for the "unfettered proclamation of Yeshua," I see this as deeply connected with what I've described above. From my perspective, gospel proclamations that have been divorced from the Jewish context of Israel's Messiah and his mission have been one of the most destructive patterns in terms of Messiah's revelation reaching the Jewish people. Proclamation of a gentilized Jesus stripped of his distinctive Jewish nature and work has continually blinded our people to the reality of their Messiah. As your mother (of blessed memory) used to say, echoing the Joseph story, it's as if Yeshua has been sold to the nations and dressed up in foreign garb that makes him unrecognizable to his own people. I believe this is one of God's great purposes in bringing the Messianic movement back into existence in our day—that we might proclaim our Jewish Messiah to the Jewish people in a way that is no longer foreign and alien to them. We are able to live out the vision of the messianic era within the Jewish world, demonstrating that indeed Israel remains at the heart of God's redemptive mission.

To speak personally for a moment, our family is very close with the local Chabad rabbi and his family. My husband prays every Shabbat with the Chabad community, we celebrate holidays and life cycle events with them, and we consider them to be among our closest community. In our case, this kind of fellowship is made possible by the fact that we share the same rhythm of life and the same values and priorities regarding the significance of Jewish identity. They have known from the beginning that we are believers in Yeshua, and all of the material they have been provided by so-called "anti-missionaries" does not apply to us; we are not Christians whose goal is to bring them into the church and thereby away from their Jewish identity and observance. We believe and hope that our presence in their lives will increasingly create an uncomfortable cognitive dissonance for them, perhaps one day leading them to question whether Yeshua might be more than the object of Gentile idolatry that they have assumed him to be.

I believe I am now in a position to address the alleged inconsistency you have perceived in my letters. You are correct that my view on these matters is theologically derived and theologically driven. However, I do not see it as inconsistent or impossible to share a set of core practices with those whom we have serious theological disagreements. For example, why should circumcising our sons on the eighth day look any different for us than for the Chabad family I just described? Why should hearing the shofar blown on Rosh Hashanah look different for Messianic Jews than for non-Messianic Jews? Why should our fasting on Yom Kippur be different than theirs? In my view, there is a set of core practices that can be observed despite our diverse (and in some cases contradictory) theological perspectives.

There are, of course, other practices that will be determined by our theological differences. For example, I believe it is incumbent upon the Messianic movement to develop coherent Jewish practices for rituals such as *tevilah* (baptism) and *zichron maschiach* (Eucharist).[1] These will be the unique practices of our communities, and they are indeed born out of our specific theological commitments.

There is another set of commandments regarding which our community will inevitably represent a spectrum of observance based upon the unique contexts of individuals and individual communities. For example, especially for those living in the diaspora, one's practice of *kashrut* is likely to be more flexible in order to accommodate the kind of unity we both agree is paramount in the new covenant. However, this should not necessarily lead to a wholesale departure from halakhic *kashrut* standards. I might choose to eat in the home of a Gentile family in order to place a rightful priority on table fellowship, but that does not mean that I must eat *treif* in that context, or any other.

For me, this range of practices (those that can be shared amidst theological diversity, those that are unique to our community, and those that must be flexible in order to uphold the particular concerns of the New Testament) represents what it means to be committed to Jewish observance and yet guided by the Spirit in one's halakhic commitments.

With regard to your stated goals in terms of your personal ministry, I absolutely applaud and support the pillars you have described. However, from my perspective and with regard to my own personal ministry, I don't believe any of these goals can be carried out in a way that is neutral to the Jewish identity I've received, and the Jewish Messiah I follow. My identity as a follower of Yeshua is inseparable from my identity as a Jew, and despite endless difficulties and obstacles, I see my mission and witness as pressing forward in forging together these two central aspects of my identity that the world would tell me are incompatible.

---

1. The Messianic Jewish Rabbinical Council has in fact been working on developing uniquely Messianic Jewish rituals for these rites. See www.ourrabbis.org for more details on the MJRC's work and for access to the Standards of Observance that this body has produced.

January 6, 2018

On a larger scale, I see this as the calling of our entire movement. In this way, I believe our movement has a commission that is distinct from the non-Jewish branch of the *ekklesia*. In the same way that we as individual Jews are called to maintain and honor the covenant that God made with the people of Israel while pledging our loyalty to Messiah, I believe that our movement has been brought into existence to make such a reality visible to the world at large. In other words, I see it as part of our calling to reject the dichotomy between Torah and Messiah that both Jewish and Christian tradition have foisted upon us for centuries. My view of a bilateral ecclesiology thus corresponds to a bilateral missiology—while the Gentile church must shine the light of Messiah into a dark and twisted world, we must also serve as a reminder that the Savior of the world is indeed Israel's Messiah, and that Yeshua's means of redemption have always been made manifest according to the terms of the ancient covenant forged between God and Israel, now extended to the nations through the work of Messiah.

Finally, regarding your Christological questions, my Christology is every bit as high as you suspect, though my words may fumble in expressing this. My sense is that the deeper issue at play here is that I do not see Messiah stepping away from the framework of Torah, but rather revealing its true meaning, power and beauty. Yeshua's submission to Torah in no way diminishes his status as the image of the invisible God, in the same way that his undergoing baptism does not diminish his sinless life. Rather, it clearly reveals the theological matrix that he comes within, a matrix that has always centered upon God's covenant with and work within the people of Israel. Our calling thus takes its cues from his actions.

Jen

JANUARY 8, 2019

Jen,

    Thank you for your thoughts and your ongoing ability to see and cogently reveal the heart of the issues. One thing that I have learned over my years in the Messianic movement is to be very cautious before making judgments about the way others should live. Our differences, not only from our Gentile brothers and sisters, but even within our movement, can display the brilliant inner workings of the plan of God to reveal the richness of our Messianic faith to as many people as possible. We serve a God who does not fit neatly into any religious box, and we represent him before a multifarious Jewish people. As such, I applaud the life of your family as a part of that picture. I appreciate your zeal and the fact that you have not kept your Messianic faith a secret with your associations within the Orthodox Jewish community. I pray that the witness of your family will bear much fruit.

    Having said that, it seems to me that we are not quite ready to leave a couple fundamental theological/biblical questions. First question: Are we—or are we supposed to be—the Spirit-filled, twice-born, new creations of which the New Testament speaks? That is, when Yeshua or Paul use "born again/born of the Spirit" (John 3) or "new creation" language (2 Cor 5:17), are these and other analogous terms and phrases merely theoretical goals at which to aim, or is this new existence truly possible? Judging by a statement in your first letter that asserted that even Spirit-filled believers remain in a wayward state, I think there remains a fundamental disagreement between us. For me, if there is not some line of human representation of truly transformed humanity by the Spirit, then the mission of Yeshua to usher in the fulfilment of the prophets has failed. Thankfully, there is such a line even if it was and may remain a minority of those who call themselves followers of Yeshua. Despite denying this transformed humanity, you asserted that the prophets (we discussed Ezekiel in particular) said that the Spirit would come that we might be better at keeping Torah. However, the more fundamental question remained unanswered. We discussed, and presumably will continue to discuss, the nature of Spirit-filled obedience to God. But even if we were to come to some agreement, the point would be moot because it appears that you don't believe that the Spirit has helped to heal our waywardness at all. I wonder if your conclusion in this matter is because you fail to see people (historically or presently) that you think have been transformed by the Spirit because they don't match your criteria for what that should look like, or if you arrived at that conclusion on biblical grounds. Would you be willing to walk back to this statement to any extent?

The second question can only be approached if we can come to some consensus on the first question. In case we do, I'll pose the question: Is the nature of being transformed by the Spirit consistent with Rabbinic Judaism as an authoritative system? I will not deny that your arguments are to a great extent logical and consistent; however, we aren't looking for cogent or even useful theologies unless they are firmly planted in and guided by biblical truth. I propose this: If the biblical basis for hypothesis A is stronger than the biblical basis for B, and if the two are in conflict, regardless of how much we may be attached to B, it must give way to A. There are many New Testament passages that undeniably describe the importance and character of a Spirit-transformed life while the biblical case for following Rabbinic Judaism is based on fewer and more debatable texts. In addition, there are texts that many would argue stand in contrast to the rabbinic system but none that would argue or speak against following the Spirit. Based on these facts, it seems to me that in order for the weaker biblical case for the authority of Rabbinic Judaism to continue to be a consideration we must conclude that it is not in opposition to the stronger biblical case for living according to the Spirit.

So, let us look at the nature of following the Spirit. These are the gifts of the Spirit according to 1 Corinthians 12:8–10: utterances of wisdom and knowledge, faith, gifts of healing, working of miracles, prophecy, discernment of spirits, speaking in tongues. There is the discussion of communal worship in the Spirit in 1 Corinthians 14 which states: "Whenever you come together, each one has a psalm, a teaching, a revelation, a tongue, an interpretation" (14:26b). There is prayer in the Spirit which includes "groans too deep for words" (Rom 8:26). There is the fruit of the Spirit, which is "love, joy, peace, patience, kindness, goodness, faithfulness, gentleness, self-control" (Gal 5:22–23). There is the glorification of Yeshua by the Spirit (John 15:26; 1 Cor 12:3). There is freedom in the Spirit (2 Cor 3:17). It is by the Spirit that Jews and Gentiles together form the new temple of God (Eph 2:22).

While Rabbinic Judaism would affirm some of the above (the fruit of the Spirit, for example), we are faced with two important conclusions: 1) *There is nothing in any of the above passages that necessitates Rabbinic Judaism.* That is, nothing unique to orthodox *halakha* (Sabbath rules, *kashrut*, etc.) has made the list of evidences of the Holy Spirit. This is in line with Yeshua's definition of unrighteousness in Mark 7 which also lists nothing for which rabbinism is the necessary cure; 2) *There are some things in the above lists that are at odds with Rabbinic Judaism.* Orthodox worship, for example, does not encourage everyone coming in with "a psalm, a teaching, a revelation, a tongue, an interpretation." Nor do the rabbis accept that aspect of the Spirit's leading that would honor Yeshua; neither is the spiritual unity of Jews and Gentiles in line with rabbinism. Also, one would have to have an imaginative understanding of "freedom" to say that Rabbinic Judaism would align with that aspect.

You initially denied the existence of a people transformed by the Spirit, but in our discussion in which Yeshua's proclamations about the Spirit were equated with Ezekiel's promise of the coming of the Spirit to heal our waywardness, you pointed out that the Spirit in Ezekiel helps us in our obedience to God which you saw as Torah observance. Torah observance is now, you claim, defined by the rabbis. This, I would conclude, leads us to some difficulties. First, as stated above, the New Testament descriptions of being led by the Spirit do not align well with Rabbinic Judaism, and they certainly do not necessitate it. Second, and relatedly, a Messianic Jew could theoretically exhibit all of the gifts, fruit, prayer, and worship as described of a Spirit-filled person in the New Testament, but you would be forced to deny their being Spirit-led until they were following orthodox *halakha*. You did mention there could be exceptions, but by tying Spirit indwelling to rabbinic *halakha* through the idea of Torah observance, it seems that your list of signs of Messianic Jewish Spirit-indwelling would look more like the *Shulchan Aruch* than the New Testament. This is problematic to me. Third, if we define Spirit-indwelling according to Jewish orthopraxy, then Messianic Jews by and large demonstrate much less of the Spirit than Orthodox Jews, *Hasidic* sects, Conservative Jews, and even many Reform Jews. Thus, we are left with an odd picture in which those who follow Yeshua, the giver of the Spirit, exhibit less evidence of the Spirit than most other religious Jews who deny Yeshua. Fourth, if orthodox *halakha* is defined as Torah righteousness, then there is no need of being filled with the Spirit to heal our waywardness at all. What we would need is greater devotion, greater effort, greater learning—those things that orthopraxy promotes. However, if righteousness is defined in Yeshua, if we are called to emulate the self-sacrificial love that sent him to the cross (Matt 16:24ff; Phil 2:5ff; 1 Pet 2:21ff; etc.), then I would readily proclaim my need for the Spirit. I don't need the Spirit to be more orthodox, but I do need the Spirit to die to my old nature (Rom 6) and to live in the fullness of my Messiah's self-sacrificial love.

If I am right that obedience to God for Messianic Jews is being led and transformed by the Spirit, and that this is not the same as living according to orthopraxy, then we must surrender the latter theology rather than the former. I do not mean here that Rabbinic Judaism should be seen as something to be avoided or labeled as evil. My own life is influenced by Rabbinic Judaism to a certain extent. However, we must not define it as the goal of our movement or see it as authoritative. Our theology is too distinct from Rabbinic Judaism, and the Spirit leads us to a full expression of our new covenant theology, not to an enlivened version of rabbinic theology.

I agree that Yeshua must be seen within his Jewish context, but I would accent *his* Jewish context. There is no doubt that he cannot be fully understood apart from the Tanakh or Second Temple Judaism, and even modern Judaism can provide platforms from which to reveal Yeshua in his Jewish context. How could we know what Messiah, Passover lamb, son of David, lord of the Sabbath, etc. mean apart from God's ongoing relationship with Israel? However, I would also argue that Yeshua cannot be fully understood within Judaism, Christianity, or any religious system. To make Judaism—or Christian traditions—a largely inflexible container into which Yeshua must fit is to try to pour new wine into an old wineskin. The wineskin (Judaism) remains, but it must be pliable to the profound reality of the divine Messiah and the outpouring of the Spirit (Matt 9:17). Judaism changed radically with Moses, David, the prophets, and the Babylonian and Roman exiles, why would we expect it not to radically change with something as magnificent as the coming of the divine Messiah? In regard to your questions as to why our Jewish practice should look different than orthodox practice, I would argue that it does not *need* to look different in every instance, but neither does it *need* to look the same. It needs to look like the reality of the messianic age and the outpoured Spirit of God would lead us to have it look. Our *b'rit milot*, for example, can look the same; the issue is with saying that they *must* look the same. As soon as we say *must*, it is tradition and not the Spirit that is guiding us.

The picture that I am getting from you is that Israel would change little were it to accept Messiah en masse. I gather from your letters that were Israel to suddenly believe in Yeshua they would study the Talmud with great passion, be even more zealous in making sure their kitchens were kosher, be even more careful about not carrying a load on the Sabbath, and that they would do all of this with greater love and enlightenment because the Spirit would be guiding these activities. I honestly do not know to what extent Israel will follow orthopraxy in that great revival promised in Romans 11, so I will rely on what I do know based on the teachings of Yeshua and the New Testament description of those led by the Spirit. In the day that Israel's eyes are opened to Yeshua, they will be filled with a greater love that emulates the love of the sacrificed lamb of God. The synagogues will be filled with speaking in tongues, prophecy, and Spirit-led groanings for the redemption of the world. Gentiles will be received as fellow members of God's family and will be invited to worship without restriction. Women will be allowed to

January 8, 2019

pray and prophecy in the services (1 Cor 11:5). People will receive miraculous healings, and young and old will dream dreams and see visions. Those who maintain a higher commitment to *halakha* will not throw rocks at the cars of those who don't, but will love them as brothers and sisters, for each stands for judgment before God alone (Rom 14:10).

I feel called to live and focus on this eschatological reality here and now by the Spirit that has been promised to us in Messiah. I don't hate or even dislike orthodoxy, but neither do I see it as my calling or the apex of the spiritual expression of Messianic Jews. In fact, I fear that it will take such tremendous effort to steer the Messianic ship towards rabbinic *halakha* that it will result in division and a loss of focus on those things that we are unequivocally called to in our new covenant faith. "For the Kingdom of God is not a matter of eating and drinking but of love and peace and joy in the Holy Spirit" (Rom 14:17). My misgivings about Rabbinic Judaism aside, attempts to move an entire movement in this direction may have a negative impact on the love, peace, and joy of the Spirit for the sake of a focus on what we eat and drink.

Let us be supporters of Israel and Jewish causes, let us celebrate Messiah in the biblical feasts and Sabbaths. Some will be called to greater and some to lesser observance of rabbinism as the Spirit leads. But as soon as we draw a line from Spirit to Torah to Orthodox Judaism, we are putting a weight on our movement which we cannot bear. Nor are we necessarily so called. Though Torah and orthodoxy have helped to preserve our people, biblically speaking, Torah is not what defines us as a people; it is God's covenant with Abraham that makes us a people (Gal 3). Since it is God's covenant with Abraham that identifies us, and since that covenant came before Abraham was circumcised (Rom 4), this is a more inclusive people than that which would be defined by Torah.

Your thought that Jew/Gentile unity and distinction within the body of Messiah reveals a healing of the schism does not go far enough. In Messiah there is healing between Jew and Gentile, but there is also healing between observant and non-observant Jews, between Israeli Jews and diaspora Jews, between those with a pure lineage and intermarried families, etc. To attempt to sweep all of

Messianic Judaism into one definable people by a certain approach to Torah so that the world can see God reconciling two easily delineated groups is a Herculean task that may actually flatten out the beautiful subtleties of God's program and send the message that those in the muddy middle have no place in revealing his plan of reconciliation.

I await your reply.

Shalom and blessings to you and your faithful family,
Josh

JANUARY 14, 2019

Josh,

Once again, I'm inspired by your passion for a biblically based, Spirit-filled vision for the body of Messiah. Your dedication to ministry and your shepherding of God's people is an incredible asset to the coming of God's kingdom, and I rejoice over that. Truly.

While you've brought us back around to bedrock biblical/theological issues, I think there's another force at play that must be acknowledged and unpacked. You can quote very compelling texts to me that support your position regarding the Spirit and Torah, and I can quote back to you equally compelling texts that support my position. From my perspective, what is more pressing than the number of scriptural texts each of us can amass to support our position is the *hermeneutical lens* that each of us brings to the text, and the presuppositions that each of us lays upon the text. It is a myth to think that anyone comes to the text as an entirely neutral, blank slate, and neither of us is an exception to that. So I think we need to take some time to address our differing hermeneutical frameworks, as text wars can go on endlessly without tapping into the underlying issues at play.

For me, I come to the text with the assumption that there is significant continuity between the Tanakh and the New Testament with regard to covenantal structure, plotline, and divine revelation. I hold it as a presupposition that the early Jewish followers of Yeshua held the Torah in high regard, as did Yeshua himself. In my understanding, this is what it meant to be a Jew in the first century (and, as a side note, in every century since then until the modern era). While there was undoubtedly diversity in terms of practice and theology, I subscribe to the notion of some kind of "common

Judaism"[1] that bound the diverse sects of first century Jews into a coherent whole (identifiably distinguishable from "the nations"). While I do think there was something radically new that broke into the world through the coming of Messiah and the releasing of the Spirit, I don't see it as being in diametric opposition or contrast to the ways God had already been working in the world and shaping a people to be uniquely his own. My hermeneutical lens is backed by a number of key passages; let me cite a few of them here:

1. Matthew 23:2ff—While this entire passage is Yeshua sharply criticizing the Pharisees for being "blind guides" to the people, he does not deny or challenge their authority. Instead, he states clearly that they "sit on the seat of Moses" and that the crowds and disciples "must do and observe" whatever they tell them to do. It can reasonably be assumed that the Pharisees in Yeshua's crosshairs are not those who had acknowledged him as Messiah, and yet he still assigns them authority.

2. Matthew 23:23—Here Yeshua chides the scribes and Pharisees for scrupulously carrying out certain practices (which notably, according to my understanding, were rabbinic interpretations of actual Torah commandments) while neglecting the weightier matters of the Torah ("justice and mercy and faithfulness"). Yeshua admonishes them that "It is necessary to do these things without neglecting the others," not that they should disregard the former and solely focus on the latter.

3. Acts 15—As I've mentioned before, the central question of the Jerusalem Council regarding Gentile practices is completely nonsensical if Torah observance had been rendered obsolete for Jews.

4. Acts 21:20ff.—Paul's willingness to undergo the specified Temple rite in order to make clear that he did not "teach all the Jewish people among the Gentiles to forsake Moses, telling them not to circumcise their children or to walk according to the customs."

---

1. For an excellent introduction to this concept, see McCready and Reinhartz, *Common Judaism*.

5. 1 Cor 7:17–20—Because circumcision is shorthand for Torah observance for Paul (Rom 2:25), this passage appears to universally declare that Jews are to continue living as Jews, while Gentiles (in accordance with Acts 15) are not required to live within the particular parameters of Torah.

More texts could be listed, but again, I think the more important point is to unpack and acknowledge each of our hermeneutical lenses, which can be supported by relevant texts. The above passages are key to informing my interpretive framework. The perspective I bring to the text is supported by a particular thread of recent biblical scholarship that is led by a group of Jewish scholars who read the text through a committed Jewish lens.

In contrast, (and please correct me if I am wrong) it seems to me that your biblical hermeneutic is informed by the "parting of the ways" and subsequent history. In the wake of these historical particulars, the only community left to interpret the New Testament is a Gentile Christian community that is developing in intentional contradistinction to Rabbinic Judaism and that continually reflects an attitude of disdain and disregard for the Torah and God's covenant with the people of Israel. This interpretive tradition is continually plagued by supersessionist, anti-Jewish attitudes, a bias that can be seen clearly in the writings of the Church Fathers, leading medieval Christian theologians, the Reformers, and modern theologians right up to today. It is the interpretive lens that has been bequeathed to the Western church, and it has been well trod by centuries of Christian theology. In fact, it is the default stance of most modern, Western Christians. Without this history, I don't believe it would be possible to have an interpretation of the New Testament that is so completely unhitched from Torah.

My point is this: the biblical text is not a hermetically sealed capsule of objective truth. It is, rather, a faithful witness to God's love for and commitment to his creation and his people. We do not come to the text as neutral observers, but rather as situated human beings with particular experiences, biases and perspectives. The particulars of our lives inform the way we read and understand and apply the text, and we cannot escape the context we find ourselves in and the eyes through which we read Scripture. Nor should we try. As this conversation is showing, it is the kaleidoscope of perspectives that are brought to bear on the text that sharpen and challenge us, a process that will do its work on our hearts as we seek to honor and follow God. I think it is intellectually dishonest to assume that the text can speak to us in a neutral, non-contextualized way and that our unique perspectives contribute nothing to what we hear the text saying.

Some of your statements make it sound as though if we just work hard enough, we can extract the objective and singular meaning of the text. I don't believe this is the case. I think we need to acknowledge the socio-historical context of the text, as well as the impact that our own hermeneutical lens has on our understanding of the text.

With regard to telling others how to live, I realize in retrospect that my previous letter may have come across as overly dogmatic, and I appreciate you flagging that and prompting me to clarify a few points. My desire is never to condemn anyone for the kind of life they are living or the decisions they make in terms of *halakha*. My own dear parents eat *treif* on a regular basis, and I don't see it as my job to impose my standards on them. That being said, because of the view I hold regarding the ongoing nature and covenantal parameters of God's relationship with the Jewish people, and because of the intrinsic beauty I perceive in the Torah, I do encourage Jewish brothers and sisters—whether or not they follow Yeshua—to increasingly take hold of and venture into our unique covenantal heritage. Taking on a life of observance is and should be a gradual process, and much damage can be done by taking on too much too quickly. However, I would like to believe my own life can both represent and recommend the deeply rewarding experience of wading slowly and reflectively into a life increasingly circumscribed by the ways of Torah. I have been fortunate enough to be a part of communities that have fostered and encouraged my journey in this regard, and my hope is to play a similar role in the lives of those who may seek me out for wisdom and direction.

With regard to your wonderful questions regarding what difference the presence of the Spirit makes, let me try to explain my

January 14, 2019

perspective to you. I believe that God is fully revealed in the person of Yeshua, and through his life, death, ministry and resurrection, the fullness of God's plan for redemption and reconciliation is laid bare. The Spirit is at work in the lives of Yeshua followers and in the world at large making God's self-revelation in Yeshua known and drawing the hearts of all people toward God. To speak metaphorically, it's as if those who are enlivened by the Spirit have been awakened or had their eyes opened to the full revelation of God and how his redemptive plan beckons humanity to partner with him in bringing light into our dark and broken world.

I don't believe that those who are Spirit-filled acquire any superhuman powers that prevent them from continuing to sin and fall short of the calling they've received. They (we) are still entirely human, with the same tendency to succumb to temptation and selfishness. However, their (our) lives have been transformed by the knowledge of God that we have received. In other words, I see the Spirit as bringing about more of a noetic change rather than an ontic change. How do you disagree with this description? Do you see the Spirit as the catalyst for some kind of ontological change?

If we nurture the awakening we have undergone and continue to submit ourselves to the work and leading of the Spirit, we will begin to recognize ourselves regularly in the midst of situations where the Spirit is tangibly at work, ushering us into lives that are at the service of God's coming kingdom.

The trouble I have with your assertion that only a minority of Yeshua followers are Spirit-filled is that this framework opens the door for endless speculation about who is and who isn't, oftentimes accompanied by elaborate means by which to categorize people. I have witnessed, and perhaps you have too, Christian communities where there is a clear hierarchy based upon one's successful demonstration of certain spiritual gifts. This kind of stratification and classification seems to me at least as problematic as the type of stratification based on Torah observance that you fear and eschew. Given the criteria you listed, is the Anglican Church, for example, empirically and categorically not Spirit-led because Anglican liturgy does not necessarily encourage everyone to come with "a hymn, or a word of instruction, a revelation, a tongue or an interpretation"?

To return for a moment to Matthew 23: Yeshua's indictment against the Pharisees is focused on their priorities and their neglect of the Torah's weightier matters. To me, this indicates that exhortations of justice, mercy and faithfulness are quite prevalent in the Torah, though they may go ignored and unheeded. What you explicate as the fruit and works of the Spirit bring these weightier matters to the fore, instructing the people that their obedience to God ought to highlight and prioritize this fruit and these acts. To me, this is a sharpening and focusing of the ultimate goal and purpose of Torah rather than a departure from it and an introduction of a framework for obedience that looks completely different.

I look forward to your reply.

Jen

JANUARY 24, 2019

Jen,

As always, thank you for your challenging thoughts and irenic tone. I think I'll divide my response into three focused sections.

Responses to Your Supporting Texts

I would like to offer an alternative understanding of some of the texts you cited that you believe support your position. I believe that my explanations below offer a better approach to the texts and one more aligned with the general thrust of New Testament's focus on life in the Spirit rather than an endorsement of an expanding rabbinic law code.

1. Matthew 23:2ff—It seems likely to me that this passage is not describing an ongoing Pharisaic religious/spiritual authority for Israel but Yeshua acknowledging that, in that day and in accordance with the system that Israel had at that time, the Pharisees held a certain judicial power, in line with Exodus 18, by which disputes would be settled. Similar to how Paul suggested that secular governing authorities should be followed (Rom 13:1), so Yeshua is demanding of his followers that given their juridical position, the decisions of the Pharisees held legal sway. Given the texts that either foretell the coming of the end of Pharisaic authority (Matt 21:43) or *not* to follow at least some of the teaching of the Pharisees (Matt 16:6) or not to do the works of the Pharisees (Matt 23:3), given that we are no longer in a societal condition in which the rabbis must be approached for judicial decisions, and given the placing of

authority on believers (Matt 16:19; 1 Cor 6:1–3), it seems that Matthew 23:2–3 should not be overly applied to the current rabbinic order. We must look at all of the passages dealing with Pharisaic authority and come up with a theology that encompasses all of them.

2. Matthew 23:23—Yeshua is at best acknowledging the benefit of one traditional expansion of Torah. As someone who does see value in some rabbinic developments, I would not be bothered by this interpretation. However, I would not assume that Yeshua's backhanded approval of one rabbinic injunction means that he promotes their entire approach as an authoritative institution, especially given other passages in which he acts (in John 9 he makes mud on the Sabbath, which upset many of the Pharisees; verses 14–16) or teaches (Matt 15) in a way contrary to rabbinic developments.

3. Acts 15 has already been discussed. I'll leave it to you and our readers to determine who has the better argument on the proper application of that passage.

4. Acts 21:20ff—The driving force in Paul's letters is the gospel message, even to the point that he would skip required pilgrimage festivals to the temple (Exod 23–24) for the sake of the gospel (Acts 20:31; 1 Cor 16:18; Gal 2:1). When he finally does arrive in Jerusalem, it was not for the sake of sacrificing, but for the sake of sharing the gospel with his people. Paul partook of the rite to show that he was not against Torah or Jewish customs. But because someone is not against something does not automatically mean that they are actively promoting it. His message was not anti-Judaism, but neither was his message the saving power of Judaism. His message was something greater than Judaism to which many things in Judaism point. Participating in the Temple rite shows he is not anti-Torah, but the fact that he goes to Jerusalem for the sake of the gospel and not the temple shows that Torah (in the traditional sense) was not his focus. That he participated according to advice to show that he did not teach against Torah or Jewish customs (vs. 21) does not counter my understanding. His teachings

do not counter these things, but neither did his message promote these things except to the extent that they might point to Yeshua. His message and life were about the gospel and the indwelling of the Spirit.

5. Corinthians 7:17–20—It seems to me that your understanding that "circumcision" is shorthand for Torah observance does not always hold and that the verse you referred me to may actually diminish your point. In Romans 2:25, "Circumcision is indeed worthwhile if you keep the *Torah*; but if you break the *Torah*, your circumcision has become uncircumcision." In the first part of this verse, there is a sense in which one can be circumcised and not obey Torah. Similarly, there is a sense in which the uncircumcised can keep Torah better than some who are circumcised (Rom 2:26–27). Both concepts are at play in Romans 2. Circumcision means simply a circumcised Jew on one level and it means keeping Torah on another level. What is interesting, however, is that on the deeper level the uncircumcised Gentile can be more "circumcised" than the Jew if they keep the precepts of Torah. It seems to me that 1 Corinthians 7 is dealing with the more general idea of Jew and Gentile and not Torah observance. If this is not the case, then your point is diminished in this way: verse nineteen says that "Circumcision is nothing and uncircumcision is nothing—but keeping God's commandments matters." If circumcision here means Torah observance, as you maintain, then the verse is saying that Torah observance is not equal to the commandments of God and "is nothing." I take the passage in a very general manner: when one comes to Messiah, the Jew should not actively seek to live like a Gentile, nor the Gentile actively seek to become a Jew. How one remains a Jew or a Gentile will be greatly affected by their newfound faith and the leading of the Spirit, as I have mentioned in my previous letter. It seems to me that this passage helps neither of our cases, for if we take your understanding of "circumcision" it ends up that Torah observance is "nothing" and is not synonymous with the commandments of God. If we take my understanding,

then a Messianic Jew should not actively seek to live like a non-Jew, but the passage remains too general to have it vouch for any particular method of Torah observance. And this is as it should be because the main point of the passage is not about keeping Torah but about the importance of not thinking that becoming a Jew or a non-Jew adds to our spiritual merit; our merit is found in Messiah alone.

In Response to Your Thoughts on "Hermeneutical Lenses"

I agree with you that there is great continuity between the Tanakh and the New Testament. A large part of that continuity is that the coming Messiah fulfills not just the obvious messianic prophecies, but the promises, hopes, and themes expressed in the Tanakh. Likewise, the outpouring of the Spirit fulfills Ezekiel 36 and similar passages, as has been discussed.

I would argue, however, that our main issue is not who is presenting a more contiguous connection between the Tanakh and the New Testament, but whether the type of continuity described by the New Testament is compatible with the type of continuity found in Rabbinic Judaism. Given that the New Testament is more in line with eschatologically-driven forms of Second Temple Judaism, and that Rabbinic Judaism purposely tones down such a focus, and given that the New Testament highlights the continuity of blood sacrifice and priestly functions with Yeshua's sacrifice while Rabbinic Judaism replaces the need for sacrifices with prayer, and given that the New Testament is contiguous with the Tanakh's yearning for the Messiah while Rabbinic Judaism denies that Messiah, and given that the New Testament is contiguous with the idea of prophetic utterances while Rabbinic Judaism purposely mutes that voice, and given that the New Testament is contiguous with the ideal of universal worship of Israel's God (Isa 56:3ff) while Rabbinic Judaism is largely insular, I would say that the New Testament is contiguous with the Tanakh in a way that is of a wholly other and often irreconcilably different focus than is Rabbinic Judaism. The above list shows that there are a number of ways that Rabbinic Judaism is *not* in strict continuity with the Tanakh, and many of these are matters of great importance to our Messianic faith.

Here I will answer your questions in regard to my "hermeneutical lens." I believe and hope that my hermeneutical lens is solidly Bible-based and Spirit-led, that it arises out of the text and my life in the Spirit. I do not share your pessimism for finding the truth behind many theological ideas by an honest interaction with the Bible, though I would agree that finding it is often more difficult than people realize. Not only does it take an honest interaction with the text, but it requires a willingness to sacrifice many of our most prized theological convictions should the texts consistently lead in that direction. Likewise, it takes a reliance on hearing God's voice above relying on our own intellectual conclusions. In other words, while my "lens" will color my reading of the texts, I hope that the opposite has happened first, that my lens has grown out of an honest searching of the Scriptures and my own heart with the Spirit's guidance. I believe this is possible, perhaps because I have a different view of the potential for guidance and transformation in the Spirit. It seems to me that the New Testament is full of examples in which old understandings were radically altered with new ones through encounters with Yeshua (John 20:28; Acts 9), witnessing the work of the Spirit (Acts 2; 11:1–18), and honestly searching the Scriptures (Acts 17:11–12). Likewise, the Tanakh gives examples of radically overturned presuppositions (Job 42:5; 2 Kgs 5:15). Presuppositions played no part in Paul's understanding of his Damascus Road incident (Acts 9), but rather, his previous presuppositions were completely overthrown. Honest conclusions to the biblical text must be possible, otherwise why engage in biblical theology instead of philosophy and sociology? Honest conclusions are only possible, however, if like Paul, we are willing to count all things as loss for the sake of Messiah (Phil 3:8).

And this leads me to my hermeneutical lens, which is this: all things lead to the glorification of the Messiah. I see the Scriptures pointing to the glory of Messiah and to us being found in him. So, when I consider ecclesiology, Israelology, continuity between the testaments, and pneumatology, my goal is to approach these subjects in a Holy Spirit-guided manner that glorifies Yeshua. For example, were I to limit Gentile believers in Yeshua to the role of onlooker in a marriage between Israel and God instead of as equally partnering in the identity of the bride, it decreases the glory of Messiah's work in reconciling people from all nations to God. Were I to dismiss Israel as a people replaced by the church, I limit the glory of Messiah by calling him unfaithful to God's promises to the Jewish people. Were I to say that Israel would change little in its acceptance of Messiah, I limit Messiah's glory by assuming that he brings only nominal newness in revelation and reality. Were I to say that life in the Spirit produces no radical personal change, I limit the glory of the Messiah as the one who poured out the Spirit for the purpose of transformation.

It is this concern for the proper glorification of the Messiah that colors my approach to Torah as a system. In its primary aims, that of the "weightier matters" (justice, mercy, faithfulness), Messiah brings out the fullness which the Spirit helps me to live, and in this understanding of Torah, I strive to be perfectly Torah observant. However, as a system that presupposes our failure to live up to these ideals and compensates for our hard heartedness with a plethora of rules and promises of blessings and curses to keep us in line, it must yield to the new or risk getting in the way of the work of the Spirit. And that in turn minimizes the glory of Yeshua who poured out the Spirit for the sake of transforming us (Titus 3:5). We must understand how Torah leads us to Messiah and then submits to him when he arrives on the scene. Then the Torah's primary goals and aims continue under his rulership. An approach to Torah observance which refuses to give way to the new reality becomes a hindrance and diminishes Messiah's glory. I am not anti-Torah. However, I consider the new understanding of Torah in the messianic age to be irreconcilable with a desire to continue and enlarge the system of Torah that existed before Messiah's glorification. To say that Messiah, the person so fully from God that he was himself God, should change little is like seeing a ten-ton boulder thrown into a pond and expecting the ripples of a pebble.

It seems to me that you are only seeing two possibilities in approaching Torah. One is the option of being pro-Torah and defining Torah through Rabbinic Judaism. The other option is focusing on

Torah as a necessary but negative institution that became obsolete with the giving of the Spirit. I do not fit either category. We would agree that the Spirit enables us to keep Torah. That is my position. However, in order for Messiah to be rightly glorified, he must now redefine Torah—sharpening its "weighty matters" and reworking the halakhic focus for those reborn in the Spirit. Torah is now found in him. I see no harm in a Rabbinic Jewish life for those so called, but I see a battle for authority over defining Torah, and Rabbinic Judaism must yield to Yeshua's authority. I assume that a rabbinic life, with some modifications, can exist as a subset to the greater calling in Messiah. I reject that Rabbinic Judaism is synonymous with or fulfills that greater calling. I can be the most Orthodox Jew possible, but if I deny Yeshua's sacrifice and priesthood, am I really being Torah observant according to the New Testament definition?

In Response to Your Question About Transformation in the Spirit

To answer your question about whether or not I see the Spirit as the catalyst for an ontological change: yes, I absolutely do. Yeshua's language of "rebirth" (John 3), Paul's language of "new creation" (Gal 6:15; 2 Co 5:17), Ezekiel's prophecy of a "new heart" and a "new spirit," Paul's discussion of an inheritance from the "second Adam," and my own experience have led me to this conclusion. This does not mean that I or others have perfected living in the new, but temptation has much less of a draw because a radical change has occurred such that sin is now contrary to the new nature. I don't sin less now because of greater effort but because my heart has been transformed into the image of Messiah (Rom 8:29). I desire righteousness, not because of a desire to avoid punishment or to receive adulation, but because my heart has a natural and strong love for God. "With respect to your former lifestyle, you are to lay aside the old self corrupted by its deceitful desires, be renewed in the spirit of your mind, and put on the new self—created to be like God in true righteousness and holiness" (Eph 4:22–24). Our new self is a matter of new creation, and not just new learning.

The concern about judgmentalism towards those not reborn is nullified when we remember that we are made new only by the grace of the Lord and that the very nature of this new self is in the likeness of the humble love of Yeshua. However, to remove all forms of "stratification" (as a truth, not as a ground for judgment) is also to remove all possibility of transformation from old to new. Fully exhibiting the Spirit in congregational worship as explained by Paul in 1 Corinthians 14 is, I would say, an ideal result but not the primary marker of being reborn. Rather, the marker is an enlarged capacity to love in emulation of Yeshua's sacrificial life (Matt 16:24; Gal 2:20; Phil 2:3ff; 1 Pet 2:21ff; etc.), to not only take up one's cross, but to find a joy in doing so that our old self could not understand. Determining who does and does not fit that classification is not my job. It is only my job to live it and encourage the acceptance of this new life for others. I should still love and serve those not yet born of the Spirit even as Messiah died for me while I was still a sinner (Rom 5:8).

As one who takes to heart the "new creation" language of the New Testament, it might be instructive for me to talk personally and practically about what that life looks like. The normal human approach to obeying God would be to hear God's commandments and do them. The more I learn of God and his will, the more I fear and love him and thus follow him. The more I learn of his commandments, the more I am able to obey them. How is it different for one who takes seriously the idea of being born again? I would say that these elements of learning and obeying are present in my life, but that it is not the totality nor the height of my spirituality. Obedience does not come by greater human effort but by allowing the Spirit of God to help me die to the old and live in the new. Personal and communal times in the Bible and prayer are critically important to this way of life. I think that those who truly desire to live by the Spirit often underestimate how much time must be spent in prayer, Bible meditation, and worship for the purpose of dying to our old ways and reconnecting with the truth of our new identity. Similarly, trials and temptations must be looked at as opportunities to die to the selfish nature and live in the new. The old must come off, as Paul says. For me to not look lustfully at a woman other than

JANUARY 24, 2019

my wife is not good enough. I don't want to see a beautiful woman, have my thoughts consumed with how I need to not lust, and then pat myself on the back for having self-control after she passes. That's a miserable existence. I want to be so done with the old and so alive in who Messiah has made me that I acknowledge the handiwork of God in creating beautiful people. I want to love her with no self-centered lustful intention at all. I want to pray for her, and, if possible, share the love of Messiah with her. I don't want to just do the Torah that says don't commit adultery; I don't want to just follow a rule that says not to lust. I want to be free in the Spirit to interact with and respond to the people and circumstances around me out of being remade in Messiah's image who came "not to be served, but to serve," who had no problem humbly washing the feet of his disciples, and who gave his life freely as our redemption.

My warning to those who follow the rabbinic path is not that there is anything inherently wrong with, say, avoiding eating milk and meat together or following any number of rabbinic dictates, but that there is an easy pitfall that says that in following these rules we can be pleasing to God, when true obedience to God means being made into the likeness of Messiah by the work of his Spirit. To accentuate this point, we must look at Yeshua whose highest demonstration of obedience was not Torah observance, though he did that, but rather his sacrificial death on the cross in accordance with the will of the Father. While I am not denying that all humans are capable of love, even very intense love, the ability to do so consistently with pure motives is a work of the Spirit. I do not judge to what extent the Spirit is or is not at work someone's life. My own mother, growing up in Conservative Judaism, described to me events and feelings from her childhood that sound very much like the work of the Spirit in her heart before she was able to verbalize her faith in Yeshua.[1] I don't claim to be able to look into another's

1. I am not advocating for a far-reaching theology of "unrecognized mediation" (salvation through Yeshua without explicit acceptance of Yeshua), but rather for caution in judging within whom the Spirit of God is or is not at work. The fact that God was at work within my mother was made manifest when, without ever having considered faith in Yeshua because of her Jewishness, she spontaneously answered "yes" (and meant it) when asked by a Christian if she believed in Jesus.

heart and make a judgment as to their interaction with the light of Messiah. But I can state without a doubt that those who acknowledge and truly follow Yeshua are new creations by the work of the Spirit, and that for such as these, the Torah commandments are not enough. Our Torah life is in being made like Yeshua, that is, being remade into the image of the second Adam and losing the fallen identity of the first Adam. This is, in my understanding, a large part of why God had to come as a man to save us. It's not just that our sins needed to be atoned for, but that on the cross the inheritance of the fallen Adam came to an end. For those who have been "crucified with Messiah" (Gal 2:20), the inheritance of fallen Adam is now also gone for us. Our focus is not on following rules, but on thinking and living as the new creations we are (Gal 6:15; 2 Cor 5:17).

I look forward to your thoughts.

My prayers are with you and your family,
Josh

APRIL 30, 2019

Josh,

Thank you for your impassioned exposition of the Spirit-filled life and your correlative understanding of Scripture. Here is my response.

On Biblical Hermeneutics

In response to what you have written, I need to reiterate a point I have already made and unpack it in more detail. While you may not agree with me, I contend that the reading of Paul (and the New Testament more broadly) that you have offered would not be possible without the particular history between Judaism and Christianity to which we are heirs. Most notably, the "parting of the ways" sets the backdrop for the next 1700 years or so of biblical interpretation. This irreversible schism ushers in an interpretive lens whereby Paul must have found some fault with Judaism and therefore sought to forge an alternate path to covenant relationship with God. Depending on which well of Pauline scholarship one drinks from, the flaw he found with Judaism is either its "works righteousness" system of earning God's favor (as opposed to the "grace" that is characteristic of the new covenant), or alternatively Judaism's "ethnocentrism," whereby the "nations" are somehow seen as outside the sphere of God's covenantal pursuit. This scheme then fills in the blanks accordingly: Torah becomes antiquated with the coming of Messiah, Torah was only ever meant to reveal sin, and, eventually, the new covenant people replaces the people of Israel as God's beloved.

The hermeneutical lens you offer makes no explicit reference to any of this, but I contend that it is in the air we breathe. No one comes to the text as a completely blank slate. While you seem to disagree with me, I believe that each of us holds preconceptions that influence our understanding of these passages, as well as the whole arc of Scripture. In my mind, the fact that you seem to deny such presuppositions is further proof that they exist. It is a distinctively modern evangelical perspective that one can read Scripture "alone," with no reference to the history of interpretation or the broader history of the relevant religious traditions. This individualistic approach to Scripture has its roots in the Enlightenment and closely mirrors Western notions of anthropology and meaning. In the words of Gerald McDermott, "the real question is not whether tradition influences our interpretation of the Bible, but *which* tradition."[1]

In his masterful work *Canon and Criterion in Christian Theology*, William Abraham explains that the very canonization of the New Testament went hand in hand with a parallel canonization of tradition. In his words,

> the Church deliberately set aside a particular set of books as special and sacred, as the relevant decrees make clear. What is equally clear is the fact that the Church also canonized a credal statement. It was not content to have merely a list of books. While the canon of Scripture was important in meeting certain needs within the community, it was not on its own deemed adequate to meet other intellectual and spiritual needs of the community. *For this reason it is artificial and misleading to hold that the only canonical material adopted by the Church was that represented by the New Testament.* Despite the high status accorded to the New Testament documents, the community over time took the definite decision to nominate certain doctrinal proposals as canonical alongside the New Testament. This decision has profound implications for our understanding of the canonical process of the Church.[2]

In other words, as articulated by McDermott and Abraham, Scripture and tradition were always intended to *interpret one*

---

1. McDermott, "Why You Can't Read Scripture Alone."
2. Abraham, *Canon and Criterion*, 35. Italics added.

another. When you combine this notion with the history that unfolds, biblical interpretation and tradition come to reflect Judaism and Christianity as two distinct silos that become mutually exclusive. As Messianic Jews, we must therefore not only accept and interface with church tradition, but also with what was intentionally excluded from it—rabbinic tradition. While we need not accept either as unquestionably authoritative and inerrant, we must allow both to inform our understanding of the text and of our own identity and calling.

As you are no doubt aware, the well-worn paradigms of New Testament interpretation are being called into question in our day. For example, the "traditional" interpretation of Paul whereby Paul had a radical break with Judaism after having found something superior in Christ has been challenged in recent decades, most pointedly by the "Paul within Judaism" camp.[3] It is remarkable that for the first time in many centuries, there are Jews reading Paul and the New Testament through a Jewish lens, which is bound to reveal a different portrait than the exclusively Gentile interpretive community of the past 1700+ years. We are just at the beginning of this veritable Pauline revolution, and I believe its implications will continue to gain force and momentum. The interpretive lens of this new chapter of Pauline scholarship grates sharply against the more traditional framework that is reflected in your hermeneutical lens.

On Israel and the Spirit

In order to further flesh out my position, I would like to return to a point you made in your January 8, 2019 letter. You wrote: "The picture that I am getting from you is that Israel would change little were it to accept Messiah en masse. I gather from your letters that were Israel to suddenly believe in Yeshua they would study the Talmud with great passion, be even more zealous in making sure their kitchens were kosher, be even more careful about not carrying a load on the Sabbath, and that they would do all of this with greater love and enlightenment because the Spirit would be guiding these

---

3. See, for example, Nanos and Zetterholm, *Paul Within Judaism*.

activities." While you have captured one aspect of my perspective here, your description does not represent the fullness of it.

I believe that if the people of Israel experienced a revelation of Yeshua and his Spirit en masse, they would more fully realize and embody the calling which they received long ago. That calling is not only to observe the particular *mitzvot* of the Torah, but to be a light to the nations (Isa 49:6). They are to model what it means to be in covenant relationship with the one true God, such that "In those days it will come to pass that ten men from every language of the nations will grasp the corner of the garment of a Jew saying, 'Let us go with you, for we have heard that God is with you'" (Zech 8:23).

Because the Spirit is the agent and instrument of unity between Jew and Gentile, a revelation of Yeshua to the people of Israel would lead Israel to enter into a new kind of relationship with those from the nations who also worship the God of Israel. This new relationship would reflect neither the ongoing hostility between Israel and the nations that characterizes the Tanakh, nor the ongoing strife between Israel and the nations that we see in our world today. Rather, Israel would be the world's signpost pointing to the reality of Israel's God and ushering the nations into the kind of intimate covenantal fellowship that Israel has always known. Together, Israel and those from the nations who cling to God would usher in the eschatological vision we see reiterated throughout the prophets.

According to this vision, the end goal of the spiritual life is not individual holiness, obedience, and submission to God, but rather *new creation*, whereby "the earth will be full of the knowledge of Adonai, as the waters cover the sea" (Isa 11:9). This is the prophetic vision of eschatological consummation, and Israel's part in it—as Israel—is paramount. With an explicit revelation of Yeshua, Israel's practice of Torah would fully embrace and embody the inbreaking of God's redemptive kingdom.

When you described the personal and practical dimensions of life in the Spirit, your portrayal echoes the classic Christian understanding of spiritual disciplines and their centrality in the life of faith. From my perspective, what Christians call "spiritual disciplines" is merely a Christian/Gentile version of Torah; it charts a way of life empowered by the Spirit that enables obedience to and intimacy with God. So, yes, it is the Spirit at work in us that facilitates and enlivens our obedience and discipleship. Once again, to my mind, Christians are merely mirroring a de-Judaized understanding of the Torah.

On Torah

You outline "two possibilities" of approaching Torah that you perceive in my approach, and you explain that your position does not fit into either category. My issue with your definition of Torah is that it lacks a *continuous interpretive tradition*. I absolutely agree that Yeshua reconfigures Torah, and that his precedent needs to be our model. However, as I argued above regarding biblical interpretation, our conception of Yeshua and how exactly he redefined Torah is inevitably read alongside *some* thread of tradition. The Christian tradition has provided one standard pattern of interpretation, with some variations: Torah has become obsolete in the new covenant, at least in the way it functioned in Tanakh. In other words, if we agree that Torah maintains significance in some regard as an integral part of God's covenant with Israel, the Christian world has not provided us with any map of what this might look like.

For this reason, our community needs the guidance of Rabbinic Judaism in the absence of a uniquely Messianic Jewish interpretive tradition. Again, we need not confer ultimate authority on the dictates of Rabbinic Judaism, but we need to be listening in on the conversation the rabbis have been having over the last two millennia. Without some connection to the living, breathing, historical Jewish community and its rhythm of life and worship, our own claim to Jewish identity becomes anemic and distorted.

This, then, is our calling: to navigate between the two traditions that have each definitively excluded us. We must draw out the elements of rabbinic tradition that enhance our understanding and practice of following Messiah, and reject those practices that are incompatible with Messiah. The same is true regarding church tradition: we must embrace those elements that accurately reflect the mission and character of Israel's God, and reject those elements that misrepresent God's covenant and covenant people.

I look forward to your reply.
Jen

MAY 8, 2019

Shalom Jen,

Thanks again for your thoughtful responses. I'll follow your headings, which I think are apt.

On Biblical Hermeneutics

You said: "Depending on which well of Pauline scholarship one drinks from, the flaw he found with Judaism is either its 'works righteousness' system of earning God's favor (as opposed to the 'grace' that is characteristic of the new covenant), or alternatively Judaism's 'ethnocentrism,' whereby the 'nations' are somehow seen as outside the sphere of God's covenantal pursuit." While I think that Rabbinic Judaism can be prone to both of these flaws, neither of these is the main issue for me in refusing to equate Rabbinic Judaism with Torah for Messianic Jews. Rabbinic Judaism rejects Yeshua and, as such, has not entered into the eschatological reality of the outpouring of the Spirit. Even if the Judaism of Paul's day was perfect in its old covenant practice, even if there were no fault to find in regard to its practice of Torah, its failure to enter the new reality through the Messiah is problematic. Suppose there was a stream of Judaism that adhered to the Patriarchs but rejected this new guy, Moses. Or suppose there was a segment of Judaism in the days of the early kings that rejected God's covenant with David and kept trying to crown those of the line of Saul. Didn't we enter into new eras with Moses and David such that, regardless of how beautifully aligned certain hypothetical groups could have remained to the preceding eras, to not enter that new era would have put them outside the will of God? Torah changed under David and Solomon. Worship was moved to Jerusalem, musicians were employed, the kingship and priesthood were inseparably linked. These were positive changes that Israel would have been remiss to not embrace. My problem with Rabbinic Judaism as an authoritative voice is not primarily that of finding faults and flaws, but that it has rejected the new. I cannot simultaneously say that the new and that which rejects the new are both authoritative even if God is active in a subtle manner behind the scenes amongst those in the old. To say that the Holy Spirit is at work in Rabbinic Judaism in a way that aligns it with Jewish new covenant living is something that it does not claim for itself and neither does the New Testament claim that for it. Also, I demonstrated in my letter of January 8th how the attributes of Holy Spirit fruit and worship described by the New Testament do not align well with seeing Rabbinic Judaism as the defining factor for new covenant Torah observance. If we are to align the Spirit and Torah, Torah must be redefined by the Spirit rather than have the Spirit's work curtailed because of a rigid approach to Torah.

Second on this topic, it seems that you have placed tradition in the place where I would put the Holy Spirit. I have mentioned my problem with equating Rabbinic Judaism with authority: it has not entered the eschatological age of the Spirit through the Messiah. My issue with the historical church is almost exactly identical. The church became the people of Christian tradition instead of the people of the Spirit. Both Judaism and Christendom largely refused to be the people of the Spirit that Yeshua's teachings, the book of Acts, and Paul's writings stress so heavily and repeatedly. Perhaps your concern over my emphasis of the Holy Spirit in regard to obedience is that you equate this line of thought with Christendom and equate Christendom with anti-Jewish sentiments. I do not equate Christendom with the Spirit and think that if the majority of Christians had been living by the authority of the Spirit—to which tradition would yield—the history of Christianity and Judaism would be vastly different and exceedingly better.

As for your stress on the need for a continuous tradition, I simply disagree. I'm not disagreeing with the pervasive influence of traditions, neither am I disagreeing with the often-positive role of tradition, but I do not see the necessity of or the biblical mandate for *focusing* on tradition. It seems to me that the weight that you

May 8, 2019

give tradition fills in many gaps that should be filled in by the Spirit of God instead. My experience has largely been that those academics and religious leaders who focus heavily on tradition are often the ones who have a lesser view of the radical transformation brought about by the Holy Spirit that I believe is taught by the Bible. Such a miraculous life and understanding is possible and is not dependent upon tradition. The biblical precedents for overturned presuppositions and breaking out of traditions that curtail the freedom of God, of which I named a handful in a previous letter, should not be dismissed because modern scholarship discounts the ability for humans to be influenced or radically changed by the supernatural. To take the leading of the Spirit and then box it into a tradition is to allow the Spirit to enliven a tradition. This can be positive, but it is a far cry from allowing the Spirit full sway. The fact that none of us do this perfectly is not an argument against us striving for this goal. This is not to say that the Spirit will necessarily reject all traditions, or that we will ever be without tradition, but it is to say that the Spirit and not the traditions are in charge. It is to say that the Spirit is not dependent on tradition though he may utilize traditions as he wills.

On Israel and the Spirit

My issue with this portion of your letter is not in the broad vision of a saved Israel being a light to the world as you beautifully presented, but in that you define the nature of Israel's obedience, at least in part, according to Rabbinic Judaism. I'm not against an Orthodox Jewish life for those whom God has called to live in that manner, but there must be one authority; that authority is either the Spirit or the rabbis. If the Spirit leads all of us to an Orthodox Jewish life (which I doubt because of the reasons stated in previous letters), then so be it. If the Spirit does not lead us to an Orthodox Jewish life, then so be it. If the Spirit leads some and not others to an Orthodox Jewish life, so be it. But to assume that the call of all Israel is to live a life dictated by the rabbis, to claim that this is our eschatological future and fulfillment as Israel, is not really putting the Spirit in the place of authority. Instead of the Spirit as a guide, he becomes a helpmeet to enable us to follow a tradition. So, it is the tradition that is in charge and the Spirit is its servant. To claim that the rabbis have been unknowingly following the Spirit to such an extent that they largely reveal the will of God for all Israel seems gratuitous. The methodology and theology of the rabbis does not lead me to have faith that they have consistently heard from God. The results of many of their deliberations, especially in rejecting Yeshua, also do not put me at ease.

On Torah

You are asking Messianic Jews to accept a rhythm of life based on rabbinic standards for the sake of maintaining our definition as Jews. In other words, you are asking us to accept what most Jews (since most are secular) have rejected as overbearing or irrelevant for the sake of being seen as Jewish. If a non-Messianic Jew does what most Messianics do in terms of religious observance, that is, if they have some connection with the major feasts, attend a congregation where there is at least some Hebrew, pray for Israel, avoid pork and shellfish, read the Torah portions, etc., very few would doubt their definition as a Jew even though they reject Talmud, drive a car on Shabbat, and eat milk and meat together. Only those judging from an Orthodox Jewish standard would call them "anemic" or "distorted" in their Jewish identity. How much more, then, should Messianic Jews, who not only largely follow the above minimal Jewish practices with spiritual vigor, but have faith in the Jewish Messiah and are filled with the Holy Spirit that was promised to Israel, be rightly seen as having a strong Jewish identity. Moreover, I see this concern of presenting a Jewish identity as a trap. The biblical concern is not Jewish identity, but how to love and follow the God of Israel. Identity, especially when it is wrapped up in how others perceive it, can divide our focus between obedience and appearance. Let us live our lives in vigor before God and let others see what they will see.

MAY 8, 2019

A Concern

One new topic. I want to broach this gently, but it needs to be discussed. I want to explain that it is not a reaction to feeling judged by you. Your letters and our interactions outside of these correspondences have been warm and irenic. This is a concern not out of feeling personally judged but out of concern for the path that accepting your approach might mean for our movement. It is a pastoral concern but with a deep connection to our theology of Torah.

There are at least two topics of greater importance than Torah that affect or are affected by our take on Torah. We must be careful how to approach Torah so that it does not negatively affect these greater concerns. The first of these is bearing the fruit of righteousness. Torah observance does not equal righteousness as seen by the fact that I can keep kosher and curse my brother in my heart at the same time, and by the fact that Yeshua's ultimate act of righteousness (dying on a cross) was not an act of Torah observance. So, we must ask how our approach to the lesser topic of Torah observance affects the greater issues of righteousness as demonstrated by love, joy, peace, etc. Specifically, how does it affect our brothers and sisters within our movement? My understanding of Torah and the Spirit, my theology, allows for you to live your life in an observant manner. I do not begrudge you your more orthodox approach to life, and I see no reason to deny that it is a genuine calling on your life from the Holy Spirit. However, your theology cannot do the same for me. As much as you might avoid the topic on a personal level because you are a genuinely kind person, the truth is that your theology forces you on some level to judge the halakhic lives of your Messianic brothers and sisters. I am wrong to drive my car on Shabbat, I am wrong to have only minimal liturgy in my congregation, etc. Your theology holds up the standard of rabbinic practice and makes a blanket statement to our movement that we all need to live up to it. I foresee a continued stress on this as leading to division within our movement instead of love, and bold halakhic standards instead of encouraging people to pursue hearing from God. Instead of seeing intermarriage, as one example, as a possible blessing from which to minister to other intermarried couples, or to emphasize the love within the family of Messiah, people will begin to second guess their marriage choices and pressure their spouses to convert. My question is this: what good is a Jewish identity if to get it we sacrifice our love and acceptance of one another? The uniform practice of the Messianic Judaism that you seek under Rabbinic Judaism will come with a great price and will not only alienate those who don't (or don't want to) fit that mold, but it will also diminish our witness to non-Orthodox Jews who make up the bulk of our people.

The second topic of greater importance than Torah is the character of our relationship with God. I consider Torah observance and relationship with God to be two separate issues. One can be Torah observant in a way that enhances that relationship, but since someone can have a dynamic walk with God apart from traditional observance, and someone else can be observant and not even believe in God, it goes to show that observance and relationship are not synonymous. We must ask: what does our approach to the lesser topic of Torah say about the greater topic of our relationship with God? My approach aims to say that God is personal, that He knows each individual and each situation and can guide them accordingly. It encourages patience with ourselves and others because it stresses growth that occurs over time because the essential elements to spiritual living are hearing from God, renewal in the Spirit, and loving, rather than halakhic standards and communal conformity. If someone were to ask me to sit in their home, observe their family, and give my uncensored spiritual guidance, I would not say things like, "you put the butter knife in the meat side of the sink; be more careful." I would say things like, "sit for a moment, and listen. What is God saying? Meditate on the Scriptures for a time. What is God saying?" This is the main thrust of my spiritual life lessons: submissively listening before a loving God who speaks to his children and transforms their hearts. If that family were Jewish and God wanted them to be more observant, then God can lead them to lighting the Shabbat candles and other observances. In that case, they would then be doing a tradition out of relationship and not out of communal or traditional pressures; neither would they be doing it because I told them so; they would be doing it because *God* told them so,

May 8, 2019

and it is only in this way that the lesser issue, Torah observance, leads to an enhancement of the greater issue, relationship with him.

Whether this is more Christian than Jewish is not my concern. That it is the way of relationship that reflects the personal loving character of God and his desires is very much my concern. It is this approach that enhances the role of the Holy Spirit in people's lives. It is this approach in my own life that has led to a greater love for God and greater peace in my family. Tradition takes on a more dominant role when we don't really believe that God speaks, guides, and transforms, or if we subconsciously fear that God may do so in a way that does not fit the picture we want for ourselves or our movement.

Again, thank you for your thoughtfulness and kindness in this discussion. I look forward to reading your response and comparing our closing reflections.

Shalom to you and your family,
Josh

MAY 20, 2019

Josh,

Again, thank you for your thoughts and your clear passion to see our movement grow and thrive in a way that honors God and makes his glory known. I'd like to respond to a handful of specific statements that you made.

First, you stated that "Rabbinic Judaism rejects Yeshua and, as such, has not entered into the eschatological reality of the outpouring of the Spirit." From my perspective, the reality is more complex than this. I would agree that, by the end of the first century and in the subsequent forging of Rabbinic Judaism, Yeshua had been definitively rejected by the rabbis. However, it is important to retrace the historical circumstances that were in play by this point. The nascent (Gentile) Christian movement had already developed an air of superiority toward its Jewish counterparts, and following Yeshua was declared absolutely incompatible with maintaining any shred of Jewish practice or rhythm of life. From my perspective, the track the church set off on (and to a large degree continues on today) reflects a severely marred portrait of who Yeshua is. The church's gentilized and anti-Jewish gospel would have us believe that Yeshua divorced himself from his people Israel, and that we must do the same in order to be his followers. So, we must ask: *which* Yeshua did Rabbinic Judaism reject? The Yeshua of the gospels and the New Testament or the Yeshua who was manufactured by the early church in the midst of its campaign of separation from Judaism? Consider Paul van Buren's apt description of this theological conundrum:

> The Gospel met Gentiles as a demand to abandon their pagan ways and service of gods that are not God. The Gospel met Jews, as the church after Paul's time preached it, as the demand to abandon the express commands and

May 20, 2019

> covenant of the very God whom the church proclaimed! Here is a profound incoherence that has arisen because of the lack of a proper Christian theology of Israel. The theological reality which such a theology must address, then, is that Israel said No to Jesus Christ out of faithfulness to his Father, the God of Israel.[1]

Your statement about the church failing to be the people of the Spirit and instead becoming "Christendom," the people of Christian tradition, further reinforces my point. This is the body that has been proclaiming the name of Yeshua throughout the centuries, and as you note, its message has not been consistent with the gospels nor, we both agree, the leading of the Spirit. So, how can you fault Rabbinic Judaism for rejecting the gospel as it was proclaimed by a church that failed to follow the Spirit? Wouldn't you agree that the gospel message as proclaimed by "Christendom" has been deeply flawed?

In your words, "to say that the Holy Spirit is at work in Rabbinic Judaism in a way that aligns it with Jewish new covenant living is something that it does not claim for itself and neither does the New Testament claim that for it." Again, I see this issue through a different lens. God's faithfulness to his covenant people—in spite of and perhaps especially in the midst of their failures, inadequacies and even apostasy—is the bedrock of the biblical story. God does not stop leading, guiding and revealing himself to his people, regardless of their current state of covenant fidelity. Yes, there are consequences to disobedience, most centrally, exile. But the covenant itself and God's steadfastness to it is never jeopardized. Accordingly, I absolutely believe that God has continued to guide Rabbinic Judaism even in its blindness toward Yeshua. To claim otherwise is to claim that God has not been faithful to the people of Israel, the majority of whom both historically and currently do not acknowledge Yeshua as the Messiah.

With regard to tradition, it seems we are not going to see eye to eye on this important point. I would contend that your position (and the low regard with which you view tradition) is absolutely

---

1. Van Buren, *A Theology*, 34, quoted in Kinzer, *Postmissionary*, 224.

influenced and guided by a particular tradition—in this case, the free church, evangelical, Protestant tradition. The anthem of this thread of tradition is a prevalent disregard for the tradition that came before, and your words parallel this rhetoric hand in glove. History weighs upon us heavily, even and perhaps especially when we are unaware of it.

In terms of authority, you wrote that "I'm not against an Orthodox Jewish life for those whom God has called to live in that manner, but there must be one authority; that authority is either the Spirit or the rabbis." Initially, I would like to clarify that I am not strictly advocating an Orthodox Jewish level of observance. Rather, I am making the case that Torah (as defined by the rabbis, though in some cases modified by the contours of life in the Spirit) still holds sway for Jews, including Messianic Jews. It is something that must be valued in our individual and, especially, corporate lives, as it has always been our unique heritage as the people of Israel.

Furthermore, because of my understanding of Yeshua's early followers and the community he and they sought to establish, I do not see the work of the Spirit and Torah as being mutually exclusive. Rather, I see them as closely connected and intertwined, as I have described in previous letters. As I have stated, I believe the Spirit has been guiding both church tradition and rabbinic tradition, though each unquestionably also bears the marks of human disobedience and tragic hostility toward one another. Nonetheless, our call is to discern and draw forth what is good and right rather than discard each tradition in its entirety.

On a related note, you claim that "the biblical concern is not Jewish identity, but how to love and follow the God of Israel." Again, I do not sharply juxtapose these two notions. From the beginning of Israel's calling and election, the clear guide for how to love and follow God has been Torah. While the church sees this connection as having been made null and void in Yeshua, the rabbis see it as continuing to have binding significance. Because I agree with the rabbis here, I contend that we must listen in on the conversations they have been having, as there is no other continual source of deliberation on what it means to be faithful to Torah in the changing circumstances of successive generations.

May 20, 2019

Finally, let me respond to the concern you raise. I don't believe there is anything inherent in my theological position that necessitates casting judgment on anyone. In fact, if someone experienced my statements as being judgmental, it would be a betrayal of my deepest convictions and values. In this way, I see my position as mirroring yours. Indeed each of us would advocate a different way forward for our movement as a whole or for individuals who might seek our counsel. Just as you perceive in my position some kind of judgement, the same could be said of yours. It seems that, by virtue of what you've been describing, my decision to adhere to certain elements of Rabbinic Judaism cannot but be elevating an irrelevant set of practices or majoring in the minors. In this regard, as I've said before, it's still not clear to me how Torah could merely be a matter of indifference in the Spirit. Ignatius' position seems more coherent: Torah either endures as a meaningful and significant aspect of life in the Spirit or it has been superseded by something superior and should be cast aside. I still struggle to fully understand the basis of your claims in this area.

I wouldn't chastise anyone for any particular level of observance or lack thereof. I would, however, encourage Jews to increasingly enter into the richness of the tradition that has shaped our corporate identity as a people, believing that to do so is to take steps toward God. I can't help but wonder if our differing experiences here are weighing upon our concerns and perspectives. I have not experienced judgment by those who are more observant than I, but perhaps you have? In this area I have been deeply impacted by Chabad, whose *shlichim* uphold an incredibly high level of observance and yet manage to make any and all feel welcome and embraced. Their goal is to invite others into the richness they themselves have found, and they don't seem to mind if those others drive to their events on Shabbat, check their cell phones during them, and go home to completely non-observant lifestyles. As far as I can tell, they merely want to offer other Jews a taste of Torah over and over again, and what happens after that is not their focus.

Your gloss on my position, namely that upholding Jewish identity somehow necessitates sacrificing our love and acceptance of one another, reflects nothing that I have claimed or advocated for. I see this as a false dichotomy that does not accurately reflect what I have written. You present a number of issues in a mutually exclusive manner, whereas I approach them quite differently. I absolutely affirm your statement that "God is personal, that he knows each individual and each situation and can guide them accordingly." However, I disagree with your related claim that "tradition takes on a more dominant role when we don't really believe that God speaks, guides, and transforms." In fact, I think it is often the case that the well-worn rhythms of tradition, whether they be The Daily Office in the Book of Common Prayer or *shacharit* in the traditional Jewish *siddur*, can be the ideal vehicles to usher us into the transforming presence of God. Along these lines, I don't see Torah observance as being necessarily juxtaposed to righteousness; I believe and have experienced that the two can go hand in hand.

Let me conclude there, and we will further explore these key differences between our respective positions in our concluding reflections.

Jen

CONCLUDING REFLECTIONS

Dear Jen,

I would like to thank you for engaging in this project with me. Your letters show tremendous heart, and your cogent arguments should not be offhandedly dismissed. Despite our critical differences, there are important similarities. We both accept the importance of Torah for our movement and submit its application to Yeshua's teachings and the reality of our Spirit-indwelled lives. Our definition of Torah and our understanding of the interplay between Spirit and tradition are at odds, but we have Torah and Spirit in common, and this allows for further dialogue.

I want to issue an apology. In my final letter I stated: "your theology forces you on some level to judge the halakhic lives of your Messianic brothers and sisters." This is not true. You have not used your high regard for rabbinic tradition as a tool to judge others. I humbly ask for your forgiveness in this matter.

However, I struggle to understand your own assessment of the importance of Torah observance for Messianic Jews. If Torah observance is merely something that "*can* go hand in hand with righteousness" (my emphasis), if you feel you are only called to give people a taste of traditional living and leave the rest to them, if using rabbinism as a standard for judging is anathema to you, I wonder if you really consider rabbinism as Torah observance in a traditional sense and in the way that most people would understand it. The Torah was *the* standard by which Israel was to be judged, yet you don't want to give what you consider to be modern Torah observance (rabbinism) that authority. In contrast, I find a life in the Spirit as the line for evaluating righteous living and the standard by which we should lovingly hold one another accountable. I think we can both say "You *should* be living by the Spirit. You *should* be bearing the fruit of the Spirit." Even if we are gentle and understanding in our approach to these matters, it is right to live by the Spirit and wrong not to do so. Your interaction with rabbinism is, apparently, not like that. If you can say "You *should* be following the Spirit," but not "You *should* separate milk and meat," then is Torah observance a secondary issue for you? In some way are you, like me, also defining Torah observance according to the Spirit if the things of the Spirit can come with a strong ought-ness to them and the things of tradition come with gentle encouragement for one's consideration? You accuse me of a more Gentile Christian approach when it comes to personal calling in distinction to communal calling, but your approach to the very thing you consider Torah is apparently not a matter over which we can hold others accountable. This seems at least as much based on personal choices as my own view. I must admit that, despite our conversation here, I am still unsure of what rabbinism is to you. It is not righteousness, even if it often overlaps with it, yet it is Torah observance. It is not a dividing line or strict standard for the community, yet you consider it a primary issue. I applaud the triumph of love over judgment in your life, but I am confused by your refusal to use rabbinism as a standard of righteousness over which to hold others accountable while simultaneously equating it with Torah observance.

I feel that most of the questions directed towards me have been answered; however, there is one issue I would like to address again. Contrary to what you stated, Torah for me is quite meaningful even if the form it takes in the new covenant is different than that of Rabbinic Judaism. Indeed, there are vital areas of discontinuity between Rabbinic Judaism and the Pentateuch, discontinuities from which my view does not suffer. Rabbinic Judaism believes that prayer has replaced sacrifice, that the voice of prophecy—the very voice with which Torah speaks—has been silenced, and that the one to whom the Torah points has not come. For both sides, Torah has transmogrified to fit modern realities, not the least of which are Messiah's coming and the Temple's destruction. However, I submit that the heart of Torah carries on more strongly through Yeshua's teachings and the Spirit's guidance than it does through rabbinism, even if my approach allows for greater flexibility in how one honors specific *mitzvot*.

Concluding Reflections

Another question in your last letter was this: "How can you fault Rabbinic Judaism for rejecting the gospel as it was proclaimed by a church that failed to follow the Spirit?" If my point was to place blame, I would have judged those claiming to be Christians while hating Jews more harshly than the rabbis who suffered under their inexcusable persecution. Perhaps my use of the word "rejection" is only applicable to that first generation of those who did so while knowing that Yeshua was not a Jew-hating deviant. However, whether through rejection or ignorance, the Jewish sages did not have Yeshua. My point was not to find fault, but to ask how we can lift up Rabbinic Judaism as a model for our movement when the rabbis have not entered through Yeshua into the age of the Spirit? Your response that God remains faithful to Israel is beside the point. God's faithfulness to us in our waywardness means that he loves us, preserves us, and will return us again to himself. It does not mean that we are necessarily teaching righteousness. The biblical record bears this out.

I would like to take what space I have left to speak about what I feel is the main issue, that is, living and worshiping in a way that rightly and fully reflects our new covenant identity. After describing himself as a Jew *par excellence*, "a Hebrew of Hebrews" and blameless in regard to Torah righteousness, Paul states:

> But whatever things were gain to me, these I have considered as loss for the sake of the Messiah. More than that, I consider all things to be loss in comparison to the surpassing value of the knowledge of Messiah *Yeshua* my Lord. Because of Him I have suffered the loss of all things; and I consider them garbage in order that I might gain Messiah and be found in Him not having my righteousness derived from *Torah*, but one that is through trusting in Messiah—the righteousness from God based on trust. My aim is to know Him and the power of His resurrection and the sharing of His sufferings, becoming like Him in His death— if somehow I might arrive at the resurrection from among the dead. (Phil. 3:7–11)

I have wrestled long and hard as both a cantor and a rabbi with the issues we have discussed. For most of that time, you would have approved of my approach even if the end result fell short of orthopraxy. I aimed for a decidedly Jewish spiritual expression. Traditional prayers and practices were the backdrop from which I worked. I departed from those only when they seemed incongruous with Yeshua's teachings, the Spirit's leading, or the congregation's attention span. Our services were heartfelt and genuinely spiritual. I would not protest if other congregations follow this model.

What I didn't realize, however, was that there was a deeper level of spirituality to which God was calling me, in which I wasn't asking the Spirit to give input on an almost fully formed script and then to bless the presentation, but one in which I was relying on the Spirit to set the agenda. I am still growing in this, but the results so far have been exciting. Words of prophecy are a regular occurrence at my congregation. We have had instantaneous healing miracles. Our ministry has branched out to include a fruitful prison ministry and a school for regular education and special needs students. The success story of the school alone is filled with miracles. We have led a handful of Jewish people to faith in Yeshua. Our services, while less traditional, vibrate with God's love for Israel. I feel so in tune with God in personal and communal prayer that I physically feel his nearness.

Despite all of this, there was still within me a draw to go back to a more traditional, less charismatic approach. The desire to look Jewish and to be appreciated as such has a tremendous attraction to me as does the nostalgia of Jewish forms. However, God spoke to me clearly through Galatians: "For if I rebuild the very things I tore down, I prove myself to be a law-breaker. For through law I died to law, so that I might live for God" (Gal 2:18–19). Whether that passage can be applied in every congregation the way that God applied it to me is not for me to say. But my understanding from the Lord was not to go back to a focus on tradition. We are not without both Jewish and Christian traditions, but they are not our focus. I had changed our focus for the sake of relying on the Spirit. I had to be like Paul and consider all else as loss in my pursuit of Yeshua.

Messianic theologian Dr. Michael Brown gives a predominantly positive assessment of Messianic Judaism, but he also recounts a prophetic warning that God had given him: "the Holy

Concluding Reflections

Spirit said to me . . . the whole Jewish temptation [by which he means a fascination with the garb and traditions of Rabbinic Judaism] . . . will fascinate, stimulate, complicate, suffocate, so be on your guard."[1] In different terms, this is what God was telling me. I was stimulated by rabbinism, but it was complicating the issue of seeking God and keeping me from a fuller spirituality. I am not prescribing Dr. Brown's message or my own Spirit-led path for all of Messianic Judaism, but I am relating these as issues to be considered carefully.

Are we rightly revealing God's character and our relationship with him through Messiah when our services are governed by hundreds of pages of pre-scripted prayers and halakhic concerns? Some argue that this is rightly honoring God's majesty, that a more casual approach is irreverent. Were we still gathered at the foot of Mount Sinai, I would agree. But at the foot of the cross in which the doors to God's presence have swung widely open, in the wake of the resurrected life to which we have been invited, I would argue that such concerns can be counterproductive. The message that many will receive through an emphasis on traditionalism is that God must be approached not just in receiving the gift of Yeshua's sacrifice, but through formalized religious practices. For many, the message of a highly scripted worship and life says that the greatest divine revelation is still the burning mountain of the unapproachable God rather than the gift of the cross, that we are those who stand in fear at Mount Sinai rather than those who boldly ascend Mount Zion with rejoicing (Heb 12:18ff).

I am painting with a broad brush. There are streams of observant Judaism that rejoice with great heart. For some, a highly scripted service and life do nothing to diminish their attachment to God. I am *not* saying that such an approach is wrong for all, but I am saying that this is not the normative and natural expression of the outworking of our theology for many people, including many Jews. Thus, a theology that says that all Messianic Jews should strive for greater scriptedness in our lives and worship may diminish the joy of our new covenant expression for those not so predisposed.

1. https://www.youtube.com/watch?v=zgQl5ajAjNo&t=12s

At the Foot of the Mountain

"One thing have I asked of *Adonai*, that will I seek: to dwell in the House of *Adonai* all the days of my life, to behold the beauty of *Adonai*, and to meditate in His Temple" (Ps 27:4). While it comes with its own traditions and baggage, the truth is that the Pentecostal/charismatic movement strives for a simpler approach to God than Orthodox Judaism and mainline churches. And despite its sometimes flaky teachings and worship expressions, I believe that the simplicity of trying to focus on God alone is why this spiritual expression is now the fastest growing movement of Yeshua in the world as well as in Israeli Messianic congregations. I believe that God is blessed by a simple, reverential approach that reflects the joy and intimacy we have with him because of the cross.

I don't purposefully eschew Rabbinic Judaism, and I could recount a number of areas in which it has a positive and continuing influence on my life. However, my identity as a Jew in Messiah doesn't need additions that are foreign to the way I was raised. If excessive tradition stifles my congregation's spiritual expression, we should not be burdened by it. If the lifetime it takes to properly pore through Talmudic literature detracts from an undivided focus on God, then it is not the right direction for me.

Your concern about a Jewish identity for our movement is answered very simply even if with less specificity than you would like. The Spirit of God loves Israel and the Jewish people. The Spirit of God will not lead us in a way that diminishes this. But neither is the Spirit of God content with Israel as she stands. She, like Paul—and like you and me—must be transformed. This transformation does not leave our approach to Torah untouched, as the New Testament makes clear. The Spirit, rather than the religious world, must define what Judaism and righteousness should be for us. As much as the idea of marrying the orthodoxy of the church and the orthopraxy of rabbinism may appeal to us, that Rabbinic Judaism cannot define for us what a Spirit-led Judaism looks like is clear from the fact that the functions of the Spirit in the New Testament do not align well, and sometimes not at all, with Rabbinic Judaism. Likewise, the institutional church has largely missed the boat by replacing an emphasis on Spirit-indwelling with an over-emphasis on creeds and sacraments.

Concluding Reflections

So, what is the way forward for our movement? *Messianic Judaism must remain Yeshua-centered, Israel-positive, and Spirit-led as we seek to live transformed lives for the glory of God.* I truly believe this is enough to keep us unified and moving forward. A listening ear, a humble heart, an open Bible, and understanding that no cow is too sacred to be kept from the sacrificial fire are the requirements for being truly and fully Spirit-led. This will lead to a Jewish expression in Messiah that is natural and God-pleasing for each individual community, and one that rightly honors the most important aspects of our faith in those foundational issues that unite us: salvation through the Jewish Messiah, lives transformed by the Spirit, and reflecting God's love for Israel and the world. In this vision there is room for the more and less traditional among us to brightly shine the love of Messiah as we unite, despite our differences, around these central matters. An overarching theology that attempts to steer our entire movement towards greater orthodoxy may place an unnecessary burden on those not so called and create a division between the more and less observant by emphasizing what divides us rather than what unites us. The fact that we can be a single movement despite our halachic differences is not a detriment that needs to be fixed; it is a beautiful testimony to the unifying power of our renewed lives in Messiah. Our multifaceted nature glorifies Yeshua and allows us to testify to Jews of all stripes. Your more observant approach is a part of the color of our movement, but I do not agree with a theology that would strive to make it the only color of our movement.

Thank you for the engaging conversation and challenging thoughts. I applaud your commitment to and genuine love for our movement and the people of Israel at large, a love that comes through in the beautiful rhythm of your family's life and the conviction of your teachings.

Your brother,
Josh

At the Foot of the Mountain

Josh,

It has been a wonderfully challenging and sharpening exercise to engage in this conversation with you, and my hope and prayer is that our words will provide a valuable resource to anyone who deeply values these issues and questions as we do.
Some final thoughts:

1. I think the Messianic Jewish movement needs to hear both of our positions and perspectives and I do not see them as being inherently mutually exclusive, even if they certainly reflect differing positions on key issues. While I clearly believe that the movement needs to consider anew the relevance and richness of rabbinic tradition, I also believe strongly that the movement needs to consistently emphasize the leading and authority of the Spirit. In fact, I would argue that our Torah observance *must* go hand in hand with our submission to the Spirit. In this regard, I deeply appreciate your concern that we daily seek the Spirit's reign in our lives and in our movement. We need a reminder of the Spirit's power and sovereignty, which you have beautifully expounded.

    It seems that your main objection to Rabbinic Judaism is the fact that it is not explicitly Spirit-led. In this regard, I think the clarion call of our movement is to be faithful to God's call upon the people of Israel, i.e., Torah, in a way that prioritizes the Spirit's leading. In making this claim, it is clear that I do not juxtapose these two foci in the way you do. In fact, I believe that a Spirit-led approach to Torah counteracts the very critiques you level against the rabbis. In the end, I think a synthesis of our two positions is what the movement needs most.

    I have been continually dismayed by the lack of resources available on a Messianic Jewish pneumatology. As with other central Christian doctrines, I believe it matters a great deal to construe pneumatology in a way that includes sustained reflection on God's covenant with Israel and its ongoing validity and significance. One of the things I most appreciate about our correspondence is its deep inquiry into life in the Spirit from a distinctively Jewish lens. In this regard, perhaps

Concluding Reflections

this book lays the foundation for a uniquely Messianic Jewish pneumatology.

2. One thing that has struck me throughout this correspondence is the difference in our primary professional roles. My primary role is academic, while yours is pastoral. There are certainly areas of overlap between these two spheres, but their central goals and means are quite different. While I recognize and value an aspect of discipleship in my teaching, my primary role is to challenge students to think deeply about ideas and their implications. By contrast, it seems to me that your primary role is to shepherd congregants through the life situations they are facing in a way that honors God. Again, these roles are and should be complementary; nonetheless, their nature and focus differ. I wonder, how has this difference between our current vocations impacted our perspectives and emphases? I imagine that you are confronted daily with people who are wrestling through the tensions that may be caused by intermarriage, significant life decisions, troubled relationships, etc. I, on the other hand, am daily confronted with Christian students who generally reflect theological claims and beliefs that are deeply supersessionist. Your task is to prayerfully counsel those who face a variety of challenging life circumstances, while mine is to unearth the theological landmines that stem from traditional Christian claims that seek to undermine Israel's election.

Because I see the election of God as deeply intertwined with the command of God, to use Karl Barth's language, I cannot but press my students on what the election of Israel actually means. In calling a specific people to be God's covenant community, God has bestowed upon this people a specific calling and commission. Thus, from my perspective, the ongoing election of Israel necessitates the ongoing practice of Judaism. As we've discussed, this claim is firmly linked to my belief in the theological significance of an ongoing distinction between Jew and Gentile.

I recognize that to make these claims in a congregational setting is quite different than making them in an academic setting. The potential implications of such claims confront you daily in the lives of actual believers, whereas my proposals are often entertained on an intellectual level by those who are not directly impacted by them, i.e., my majority Christian students. For my audience, it means a significant shift in theology; for your audience, it potentially means a significant shift in practice. While I believe both need to be addressed, I am aware that there may be more at stake in your words from the pulpit than my words in the classroom.

3. In at least one place in your letters, you seem to equate my position with advocating for an "Orthodox Jewish life." I realize you may not be the only one to make this connection, and I'd like to address it in more detail. My main point is that Torah, as defined by the rabbis in the absence of a distinctly Messianic Jewish interpretive tradition, holds ongoing significance in the lives of Messianic Jews and the Messianic Jewish movement as a whole. Without it, we lose any sense of meaningful connection with *am yisrael* and the specific calling that God has issued to our people. From my perspective, this calling is part and parcel of Israel's election.

While this may manifest itself in an Orthodox Jewish level of observance, my sense is that this will not be its primary manifestation. Rather, my hope is that Messianic Jewish individuals and groups would begin taking steps in the direction of engaging Torah observance, and that they would discover a rich oasis of spirituality in doing so. Because God speaks and works intimately in the lives of individuals, what this looks like specifically (and where the starting point is) will vary greatly.

It is also important to note that the particular life circumstances of individuals and groups of Messianic Jews will bear upon what this engagement with Torah might look like. For example, living in diaspora often presents practical difficulties with high levels of observance. These difficulties should be acknowledged and, in many cases, honored. However, such limitations rarely warrant a wholesale dismissal of Torah and its relevance.

Concluding Reflections

Let me share a particular example from my own life. When I was in graduate school, I was beginning my own foray into the world of Torah observance. I lived in a predominantly Christian community at the time, and the nearest Messianic congregation was clear across the city of Los Angeles from where I lived. I found that a higher level of observance regarding Shabbat actually further isolated me from the very community I sought to invest in. If I refused to drive on Shabbat, I was cutting myself off from meaningful and life-giving Messianic Jewish fellowship. By the end of my time there, I did seriously consider moving closer to the community, but for a number of reasons such a move was not feasible. So I chose to make an accommodation, recognizing that the greater good was community. I would not, however, advocate this as the ideal situation. It was merely an example of clashing convictions, and I have no regrets about the decision I made given the limitations I faced at the time.

Furthermore, it is important to recognize that different individuals and groups have different callings relative to both the Jewish and Christian worlds. Here I think it is especially helpful to reference a spectrum that Mark Kinzer charts. According to Kinzer, "all of the Jewish followers of Yeshua portrayed in the Apostolic Writings lived as full members of the Jewish community. However, they did so in different ways, depending on their geographical location and their particular calling."[2] For James and the Jerusalem community, immersion in Jewish rituals and rhythms of life was complete. Their primary locus of activity was the Temple, and their contact with non-Jews was likely quite limited. Paul, on the other hand, along with his Jewish colleagues, spent most of his time away from the Jerusalem community, preaching Messiah in predominantly non-Jewish areas. It is clear, however, that he perceived his "Gentile mission" to be closely connected to Israel's life and redemption. His intimate ties to the Jewish community and Jerusalem in particular remained strong

---

2. Kinzer, "Messianic Jewish Community," 20.

and central throughout his far-flung journeys. Peter seems to occupy a middle space between James and Paul, in that he is initially focused exclusively on the Jerusalem community yet eventually becomes a key figure in the proclamation of Yeshua among the Gentiles.

This New Testament spectrum is a helpful matrix for our own context as well, and the range of callings reflected in the lives of the apostles holds true today. Accordingly, one's approach to and level of Torah observance will be in direct correlation to their particular circumstances and calling. That being said, as we see with the apostles, a meaningful connection to the Jewish community functions as a baseline for Jewish followers of Yeshua. Israel is our people, though our vocations and life particulars will undoubtedly color what this actually means and looks like.

4. Another significant difference in emphasis has struck me in our correspondence: you repeatedly seem to be more concerned with the lives and decisions of individuals whereas I am more concerned with a corporate and collective identity and calling. Though you have resisted categorization along the lines of "Jewish" or "Christian," my position seems to clearly elevate the *people* of Israel, while yours emphasizes the unencumbered individual freedom and flexibility that tends to characterize evangelical, Protestant thought. In fact, it would seem that each of our overarching positions actually depends on our respective emphases; Jewish corporate identity cannot be forged if each individual Jew operates independently, and the Spirit may not be afforded the kind of freedom you seek to safeguard unless it is allowed to manifest itself in very different ways for different individual believers. As would be expected, the implications ripple outward from this central difference in fundamental orientation.

While you often speak of your vision for the future of the Messianic Jewish movement, your focus on the individual—and the different ways that the Spirit may be leading individuals with regard to Torah—makes it difficult for me to see how

Concluding Reflections

your position casts a unified vision for the future of our movement. It seems more like a vision for a very diffuse and diverse movement, which is largely what we see as the current form of Messianic Judaism. The strength of your position is that it readily allows for such diversity. But on the other hand, this level of diversity seems to undermine a united vision for the way forward.

Because I strongly believe that Messianic Judaism is a subset of Judaism and not merely a form of Christianity donning Jewish accessories, my vision for the future of our movement operates according to the contours of Jewish peoplehood, however variously this may be construed. While I strongly uphold deep and defining bonds between the Messianic Jewish movement and the larger Christian community, the focus of my vision for our movement is one that grounds it in the soil of Israel's covenant with God, circumscribed by the covenantal particulars that have always rooted Israel's corporate life and identity.

May God continue to bless and guide you as you faithfully shepherd his people.

ADDENDUM: TWO VIEWS ON TORAH IN MATTHEW 5:17–20

Do not think that I came to abolish the *Torah* or the Prophets! I did not come to abolish, but to fulfill. Amen, I tell you, until heaven and earth pass away, not the smallest letter or serif shall ever pass away from the *Torah* until all things come to pass. Therefore, whoever breaks one of the least of these commandments, and teaches others the same, shall be called least in the kingdom of heaven. But whoever keeps and teaches them, this one shall be called great in the kingdom of heaven. For I tell you that unless your righteousness exceeds that of the Pharisees and *Torah* scholars, you shall never enter the kingdom of heaven!
Yeshua (Matt 5:17–20)

Torah Under Messiah's Authority: Joshua's View

1. A literal approach to Matthew 5:17–20 is not necessary and, as will be seen below, is not possible. Yeshua often spoke in hyperbole and other shocking ways to heighten the starkness of his points (see Matt 5:29–30; Matt 15:26; 19:12). This is one of those cases.

2. A literal view that equates "the least of these commandments" and "righteousness" with the 613 commandments of the Torah or with Rabbinic Judaism does not align with the rest of the Sermon on the Mount or with Yeshua's teachings in general. That is, unless used as a springboard for another point about spirituality or morality, Yeshua avoids discussions of exacting *halakha* (Mark 7). There is no discussion of how far one may walk on the Sabbath, no recording of him denouncing those

Addendum: Two Views on Torah in Matthew 5:17–20

who fail to keep strictly kosher, no weighing in on the calendar disputes of first century Judaism, etc. Rather, his focus is continually and predictably on matters of spirituality and morality. In the Sermon on the Mount, the areas of concern include anger, unity amongst brothers, divorce, honesty, love, hypocrisy, relationship with the Father, not judging, etc. Moreover, Yeshua's typical denunciation of the Jewish religious elite in his other teachings rather than taking aim at the *am haaretz* (commoners), though the former were more punctilious, shows that his concern is not on an exacting *halakha*.

3. A literal view that equates "the least of these commandments" and "righteousness" with a literal approach to Torah or with rabbinic *halakha* presents a major theological inconsistency. Yeshua says that "For unless your righteousness exceeds that of the Pharisees and *Torah* scholars, you shall never enter the kingdom of heaven!" The conjunction "for" (γὰρ) connects "righteousness" here with what came before it, namely, "the least of these commandments." If the "least of these commandments" and "righteousness" means keeping the 613 commandments either literally or through rabbinic explication, then it follows that such is necessary for entering the kingdom of heaven. However, such an exacting approach is never the method for entering the kingdom of heaven in Yeshua's other teachings (see especially, Matt 18:3–4). If it were meant literally, then Yeshua is unequivocally teaching a works-based righteousness and Yeshua and Paul's emphasis on faith and the need for Yeshua's atoning death would then be nullified: "for if righteousness comes through *Torah*, then Messiah died for no reason!" (Gal 2:21b). In other words, we cannot use Matthew 5 as a case for covenantal nomism (obedience as a reaction to having received salvation) because Yeshua makes "righteousness" a requirement for *entering* the covenant. The righteousness he speaks of here is a matter of quality (righteousness that proceeds from a pure heart) and not quantity (how many laws are obeyed).

4. A view that equates "the least of these commandments" and "righteousness" with a literal approach to Torah or rabbinic *halakha* misses the main point of the Sermon on the Mount, which is Yeshua's authority. The subsidiary point is what accepting his authority means for one's actions, attitude, and prayer.

That the main point is Yeshua's authority is seen in the following ways: First, when comparing 5:10 with 5:11, we see that Yeshua is equating being persecuted "for the sake of righteousness" with being persecuted "on account of Me." That is, following Yeshua and being persecuted for it *is* being persecuted for righteousness. Second, Yeshua counteracts popular sayings regarding Torah by saying "you have heard it was said . . . but I tell you" with an emphatic "I."[1] Third, Yeshua teaches others not to judge (7:1) but reveals himself as the ultimate judge (7:21–23). Fourth, the *inclusio* of 5:17 and 7:12 with the terms "the *Torah* and the prophets" indicate that all of Yeshua's teachings between these two verses should be considered authoritatively revealing God's will, even though many things he said here are not direct expounding on either Torah or the prophets (his model prayer, for example).[2] Fifth, the wise man of his parable in 7:24–27 did not build his house upon the Torah, but upon the words of Yeshua! This is in contradistinction to the beginning of the *Nevi'im* (Joshua 1:8) and the *Ketuvim* (Ps 1) in which the wise man looks back to the Torah of Moses.[3] Finally, Matthew emphasizes the point of Yeshua's authority by recording the crowd's reaction, who "were astounded at his teaching, for he was teaching them as one having authority" (7:28–29).

To claim that Matthew 5:17–20 is a call to either a literal or a rabbinic approach to Torah is to void the need for the theme of Yeshua's authority. Many teachers have taught us to follow Torah and the rabbis and none needed this type of authority

---

1. Quarles, "Sermon," Kindle Locations 2486–2487.
2. Loader, *Jesus' Attitude*, 163, 186.
3. Rydelnik, *The Messianic Hope*, 67.

Addendum: Two Views on Torah in Matthew 5:17–20

to do so. To be consistent with the thrust of the text and new covenant theology, we must conclude that Yeshua is defining "the least of these commandments" and "righteousness" as being his disciple, for he alone has the wisdom and authority to properly teach and demonstrate kingdom life.

5. That Yeshua redefines keeping "the least of these commandments" in terms of accepting his authority is to use these terms in an ironic twist with an unavoidable conclusion: *you are doing the "least of these commandments" if your life submits to the authority of Yeshua as he reveals God's will and character.* The focus is different than a hyper-vigilant approach to the minutiae of rabbinic law or even Mosaic law. Matthew 5:17–20 does not answer the question of how much following Yeshua may or may not overlap with a literal approach to Torah, but we can say that the focus here is not on the rabbis or even God's revelation through Moses. The foundation for Yeshua's throne is indeed Moses and the prophets (Matt 5:17), but the new focus and revealed authority is Yeshua alone (see Matt 17:1–8). Based on later teachings, this authority is then extended to those who are his disciples (Matt 16:18–19; John 13:20; 1 Cor 6:1–4) and not to those highly observant "ruling *kohanim* and Pharisees" (Matt 21:43–45).

Torah Under Messiah's Authority: Jen's View

As we approach the Sermon on the Mount and seek to discern its meaning, it is important to note at the outset that Matthew sets up this event as a second Sinai. In Matthew 5:1, we are told explicitly that Yeshua "went up on the mountain," mirroring Moses' illustrious ascent. What follows is Yeshua's authoritative interpretation and application of Torah; he is now the model of what Torah righteousness means and looks like.

While Yeshua has repeated altercations with the Pharisees, it is clear in Matthew 5:17–20 that there is something significant, if not wholly commendable, about their scrupulous observance. Why else would Yeshua hold them up as a standard of righteousness? Pinchas

Lapide writes that Yeshua "in no way denies their righteousness, just as elsewhere (23:2f) he expressly affirms their teaching, though Jesus found it insufficient to meet his moral requirements for entrance into the realm of [the kingdom of] heaven."[4] In other halakhic disputes with the Pharisees, what is at issue is not the Torah's ongoing relevance and authority, but rather how it is to be applied and instituted (Matt 9:14–17, Matt 12:2–8, Matt 15:1–9, Matt 19:3–9, Matt 23).

Yeshua continually points out that the Pharisees' righteousness often disregards the deeper moral and ethical dimensions of the *mitzvot*. On the contrary, Yeshua's own teaching highlights and emphasizes these greater aspects of observance. Because Yeshua's kingdom is built on love, his instruction regarding Torah observance places this virtue at the core. To observe Torah in a way that is not loving to one's neighbor is a betrayal of both Torah's true meaning and Yeshua's message of salvation.

This hermeneutical lens makes sense of Yeshua's words in the rest of the Sermon on the Mount. Yeshua employs the common rabbinic practice of "building fences around the Torah." However, rather than adding additional stringencies with regard to outward actions, Yeshua raises the bar in terms of one's internal disposition and inward righteousness. So not only is murder wrong, but anger in one's heart is also "subject to judgment" (Matt 5:21–22); not only is adultery prohibited, but lust in one's heart is tantamount to adultery (Matt 5:27–28); not only is love for one's neighbor commanded, but also love for one's enemy (Matt 5:43–47). As one commentator explains, "Yeshua's words reveal the moral, ethical intention behind the commandments and expose the internal deviancy of the heart of man. He cuts past external appearances and plants the fence around Torah deep in the heart."[5]

Yeshua's words in Matthew 5, particularly in verses 17–20, are consistent with Yeshua's overall message: discipleship is all-encompassing, and fidelity to Yeshua requires one to forsake all other attachments and commitments. To follow Yeshua is to make him and

---

4. Lapide, *The Sermon on the Mount*, 21.
5. Lancaster, *Chronicles of the Messiah*, 2:475.

Addendum: Two Views on Torah in Matthew 5:17–20

his kingdom one's highest and most treasured priority, and every aspect of one's life is to reflect this orientation. Just as with Moses' Torah, obedience to Yeshua requires that every area of our lives and actions be increasingly circumscribed by righteousness and holiness. This is what it means to "be holy, as I am holy" (1 Pet 1:16, Lev 11:44–45).

BIBLIOGRAPHY

Abraham, William J. *Canon and Criterion in Christian Theology*. Oxford: Oxford University Press, 1998.
Bauckham, Richard. "James and the Jerusalem Community." In *Jewish Believers in Jesus: The Early Centuries*, edited by Oskar Skarsaune and Reidar Hvalvik, 55–95. Grand Rapids: Baker, 2007.
Carson, D. A. *The Gospel According to John*. Grand Rapids, Eerdmans, 1990.
Donin, Hayim Halevy. *To Be a Jew*. New York: Basic, 1972.
Hayford, Jack. *Living the Spirit-Formed Life: Growing in the 10 Principles of Spirit-Filled Discipleship*. Bloomington: Chosen, 2017.
International Alliance of Messianic Congregations and Synagogues (IAMCS). *The Non-Torah: Exposing the Mythology of Divine Oral Torah*. Media, PA: IAMCS, 2019.
———. "One Law, Two Sticks: A Critical Look at the Hebrew Roots Movement: A Position Paper of the International Alliance of Messianic Congregations and Synagogues (IAMCS) Steering Committee." January 15, 2014.
———. "Our Vision." http://iamcs.org/about-us/vision.
Isaacs, William. *Dialogue and the Art of Thinking Together: A Pioneering Approach to Communicating in Business and in Life*. New York: Currency, 1999.
Juster, Daniel C. "Lecture 6-2: Messianic Jewish Theology/Divine Perspective." The King's College and Seminary, Spring 2011.
Juster, Daniel C. and Russ Resnik, "One Law Movements: A Challenge to the Messianic Jewish Community." UMJC, 2005.
Kinzer, Mark. *Jerusalem Crucified, Jerusalem Risen: The Resurrected Messiah, The Jewish People, & the Land of Promise*. Eugene: Cascade, 2018.
———. "Messianic Jewish Community: Standing and Serving as a Priestly Remnant," *Kesher* 28 (2014), 79-101.
———. *Postmissionary Messianic Judaism: Redefining Christian Engagement with the Jewish People*. Grand Rapids: Brazos, 2005.
Lancaster, D. Thomas. *Chronicles of the Messiah*. Marshfield, MO: First Fruits of Zion, 2015.
Lapide, Pinchas. *The Sermon on the Mount: Utopia or Program for Action?*. Translated by Arlene Swidler. Maryknoll, NY: Orbis, 1986.
Lloyd-Jones, D. Martyn. *The Christian Soldier: An Exposition of Ephesians 6:10–20*. Grand Rapids: Baker, 1981.

Bibliography

Loader, William. *Jesus' Attitude Towards the Law: A Study of the Gospels*. Grand Rapids, MI: Eerdmans, 2002.

Longenecker, Richard N. *Acts*. In *The Expositor's Bible Commentary: Luke–Acts (Revised Edition)*, edited by Tremper Longman III and David E. Garland. Grand Rapids, MI: Zondervan, 2007.

McCready, Wayne O., and Adele Reinhartz, eds. *Common Judaism: Explorations in Second-Temple Judaism*. Minneapolis: Fortress, 2008.

McDermott, Gerald R. "Why You Can't Read Scripture Alone: Studying the Bible in Light of the Great Tradition." *Christianity Today*, November 19, 2014.

Messianic Jewish Alliance of America (MJAA). "Statement of Faith." https://mjaa.org/statement-of-faith.

Nanos, Mark, and Magnus Zetterholm. *Paul Within Judaism: Restoring the First-Century Context to the Apostle*. Minneapolis: Fortress, 2014.

Quarles, Charles. *Sermon On The Mount: Restoring Christ's Message to the Modern Church*. Nashville: B&H, 2011.

Rosner, Jennifer. "You Will Be My Witnesses: Toward a Messianic Jewish Pneumatology." Presented at the Helsinki Consultation for Jewish Continuity in the Body of Messiah. Oslo, Norway, June 2013.

Rudolph, David J. "Count Zinzendorf, Pastor Jack, and Messianic Jewish Revival." In *The Pastor & the Kingdom: Essays Honoring Jack W. Hayford*, edited by Jon Huntzinger and S. David Moore, 92–116. Southlake: Gateway Academic and TKU Press, 2018.

———. "Messianic Judaism in Antiquity and in the Modern Era." In *Introduction to Messianic Judaism: Its Ecclesial Context and Biblical Foundations*, edited by David J. Rudolph and Joel Willitts, 21–36. Grand Rapids: Zondervan, 2013.

———. "Guidelines for Healthy Theological Discussion." In *The Borough Park Papers. Symposium I: The Gospel and the Jewish People*, 7–14. Clarksville: Messianic Jewish Publishers, 2012.

———. "Reminder on Respectful Theological Discussion." In *The Borough Park Papers. Symposium II: The Deity of Messiah and the Mystery of God*, 5–11. Clarksville: Messianic Jewish Publishers, 2012.

Rudolph, Michael with Daniel C. Juster. *The Law of Messiah: Torah from a New Covenant Perspective*. Volume 1, Montgomery Village: Tikkun International, 2019.

Rydelnik, Michael. *The Messianic Hope: Is the Hebrew Bible Really Messianic?* Nashville, TN: B&H, 2010.

Snodgrass, Klyne. *Between Two Truths: Living with Biblical Tensions*. Grand Rapids: Zondervan, 1990.

Telushkin, Joseph. *Words That Hurt, Words That Heal: How to Choose Words Wisely and Well*. New York: Harper, 1996.

Tikkun International. "The Twelve Pillars." Montgomery Village: Tikkun International, 2018.

BIBLIOGRAPHY

Union of Messianic Jewish Congregations (UMJC). "Defining Messianic Judaism." http://umjc.org/defining-messianic-judaism.

———. "Statement of Faith." http://www.umjc.org/statement-of-faith.

———. "Our Values." https://www.umjc.org/values.

Van Buren, Paul M. *A Theology of the Jewish-Christian Reality, Part 2: A Christian Theology of the People Israel.* San Francisco: Harper & Row, 1983.

Zlotowitz, Meir. *Chanukah—Its History, Observance, and Significance: A Presentation Based upon Talmudic and Traditional Sources.* Brooklyn: Mesorah, 1989.

www.ingramcontent.com/pod-product-compliance
Lightning Source LLC
Chambersburg PA
CBHW070915160426
43193CB00011B/1469